Still Going It Alone

Michele Howe

Still Going It Alone

Mothering with Faith and Finesse
When the Children Have Grown

HENDRICKSON
PUBLISHERS

Still Going It Alone
Mothering with Faith and Finesse When the Children Have Grown
© 2009 by Hendrickson Publishers, Inc.
P.O. Box 3473
Peabody, Massachusetts 01961-3473

ISBN 978-1-59856-241-5

Printed in the United States of America

First Printing — January 2009

Scripture quotations are from the *Holy Bible, Today's New International Version*® (TNIV)® Copyright © 2001, 2005 by International Bible Society®. All rights reserved worldwide.

Hendrickson Publishers is strongly committed to environmentally responsible printing practices. The pages of this book were printed on 30% postconsumer waste recycled stock using only soy or vegetable based inks.

Library of Congress Cataloging-in-Publication Data

Howe, Michele.
    Still going it alone : mothering with faith and finesse when the children have grown / Michele Howe.
        p. cm.
    Includes bibliographical references (p.   ).
    ISBN 978-1-59856-241-5 (alk. paper)
    1. Single mothers—Religious life. 2. Empty nesters—Religious life. 3. Christian women—Religious life. 4. Aging—Religious aspects—Christianity. I. Title.
    BV4529.18.H695 2009
    248.8′431—dc22
                                                    2008025901

Dedication

To Jake, Alison, and Jordan Halsey
To Chelsea and Taylor Johnson
We've watched you grow into fine men and women.

(With moms like yours, it's no wonder
that you're blessings every one.)

Table of Contents

Acknowledgments

Book writing is always a community endeavor. Always. And it always begins with someone's story. A story filled with hopes, dreams, and desires . . . complicated by life's pain, sorrow, and uncertainty. But a story worth telling . . . always.

Throughout this book, I tell the stories of single moms who've been at the task of parenting for a while. Their experiences run the gamut of life's emotional, physical, and spiritual challenges and yet, despite the obstacles they face, how they respond brings me hope and courage . . . always. I thank them for that.

I also want to thank my agent, Les Stobbe, agent extraordinaire . . . your insight and experience and wise counsel mean the world to me. You're a man to be modeled after in this tough, tough business.

At Hendrickson Publishers, I feel like I've come home again. Thanks to Shirley Decker-Lucke for her enthusiastic support of this book and for catching the vision of its need in support of the ever-growing circle of single moms out there. To Sara Scott and Megan Talbot . . . you're both a joy and delight to work with. To Mary Riso . . . applause to you for getting the word out with a fervent spirit and diligent service. And, my sincerest gratitude to Mark House for his keen editorial expertise. You made it practically painless . . . and that's saying a lot. Finally, I'd like to thank Linda Grant for her editorial input on fine-tuning my work to make it a better, more useful resource.

Thank you all; your contributions will always be a warm and welcome remembrance.

Preface

 ome years ago, two of my closest friends became single moms, not by their own choice. However, these remarkable women of faith constantly made their own choices in the weeks, months, and years after their marriages ended. As their friend, I watched them choose

- *Life instead of defeat.*
- *Forgiveness instead of bitterness.*
- *Courage instead of fear.*
- *Faith-driven confidence instead of paralyzing worry.*
- *Joy instead of sorrow.*
- *Contentment instead of envy.*
- *Thankfulness instead of grumbling.*
- *Love instead of hate.*

As these women made their choices to live their new lives under the shelter and protection of Christ, everyone around them was blessed and encouraged. This was especially true for me.

This book, *Still Going It Alone: Parenting With Faith and Finesse When the Children Have Grown,* is the next chapter, so to speak, in my own attempt to address issues that are commonly faced by newly divorced moms and their families, an attempt that began with my first book, *Going It Alone: Meeting the Challenges of Being a Single Mom.*

In the same way that my dear friends learned to successfully parent solo throughout those early parenting years, they have also learned how to wisely observe the changes around them and within their families, and make appropriate changes and adjustments as their children grew up. I've watched them learn important lessons that I believe can be of great benefit to other women who struggle with the same issues. This book contains my reflections on the lessons my friends have learned as well as personal lessons I myself have learned through seeking to apply biblical wisdom to the day-to-day struggles we all face as we grow older.

In this book, you will learn more about how to adjust to the empty nest as your children move out of the home; how to impart vision and goal-setting directives to your young adult children; how to help your kids make wise relationship and marriage decisions; how to prepare yourself for a second career as well as make sound financial preparations. You'll gain helpful advice on how to joyously embrace grandparenting while simultaneously caring for your own aging parents. I'll address the complex topic of remarriage and the inevitable adjustments that go along with it. Finally, I'll share some practical advice on how to discover and maintain the precious gift of inner rest no matter what the future holds.

As my friends learned so long ago and passed on to me, none of us is meant to live life on our own. Every person, as designed by God, has a need and an innate longing for intimate community. It is my hope and prayer that this book offers single moms a safe place—a community—where they find rest and renewed hope, strength, and shelter as they travel alongside other moms on this parenting journey.

Chapter One

Entering the Crossroads

Betwixt and Between the Empty Nest

Trust in the LORD with all your heart and
lean not on your own understanding;
in all your ways submit to him, and
he will make your paths straight.
Proverbs 3:5–6

*E*ach woman thought the day would never arrive. Some dreaded it, others prayed for it. Yet every mother sees it coming, ominously lurking around the corner. The empty nest. Those who have already passed this signature mark in the childrearing process deem it another passage in life, in parenting. Others, single moms, especially single moms—those who've invested heart and soul into keeping their struggling family intact—frequently regard the thought of sending their kids off to worlds unknown as morally unconscionable. Yet like every other challenge single mothers have faced, they're determined to make the adjustment successfully, and if at all possible . . . trauma-free. Sure, there are bound to be some wrinkles in the formula. And not to forget that after years of solo parenting, these courageous survivors instinctively surpass the status quo in every possible arena of life. They've honed their coping and managerial skills to a science—nothing takes them unawares—especially when it comes to their kids.

So, as babies grow into toddlers, elementary age kids grow into teens, and high school graduates into young adults, single moms are readying themselves for the good-byes they see inching toward them. Wisely, most mothers begin making prudent plans for the upcoming "empty nest" years that won't demand so much of their daily energy and time. Mothers entering this second stage of parenting initiate a chain of events, of patterns actually, that eases both parent and child into the future with confidence. Some women realize that they've been so consumed with their children's activities; they've let the development of their own circle of social resources slide. Other moms may opt to start back to school, take up a long-neglected hobby, or rev up their volunteering pace. Step by step, single mothers from all walks of life begin putting into place small, but nevertheless significant, choices to let go of their children.

Prayerfully and systematically, the proactive mom views the future as flush with opportunity, not as an incalculable venture to be dreaded or shirked.

Prayerfully and systematically, the proactive mom views the future as flush with opportunity, not as an incalculable venture to be dreaded or shirked. Rather than grasp at the ever evolving yet diminishing relationship between mom and child, these women embrace the changes as God-ordained. Journey now with some amazing single mothers who have learned to see the good in change, expect the miraculous from the mundane, and overcome the impossible by God's good hand of grace.

Forty-eight-year-old Jennifer looked around the hastily vacated bedroom in dismay. What a mess! What in the world had Haley been thinking? Trying in vain to recall the last words her nineteen-year-old daughter called out as she darted through the door minutes earlier, Jennifer sighed . . . loud and long. Oh my. I can't leave this room in ruins for the next two months. Every time I walk past Haley's bedroom I'll be visualizing (and exaggerating) what lies beyond her closed door.

Standing akimbo, Jennifer gazed thoughtfully at the piles of unfolded clothing, the stacks of books, magazines, and assorted CDs, all apparently discarded, unwanted. Just look at this, Jennifer frowned as she reached down and pulled out a CD, a once favored collection of currently "in" pop artists. I remember the day we went shopping and Haley had to have this particular CD. When was that? A few months ago? Six? I guess it really doesn't matter now.

Jennifer stood back up and stared at the disarray glumly. What to do? Should I dutifully clean up this room and get it organized for my own peace of mind or leave it to its doom as evidence of one more lesson in life about the value of being responsible and organized? Hmmm. Stepping gingerly into the cluttered but empty—so empty—room, Jennifer decided life lessons could wait for another day. *She* couldn't stand the mess.

Okay, where to begin? I'll clear the floor first and then work the room clockwise, Jennifer decided. On hands and knees, she reached deep under Haley's bed and began exercising both her muscles and her patience. As she continued to grab and pull, Jennifer wondered just how much could be squished underneath such a small berth. What Jennifer found continued to both astound and amaze her. Not only did Haley trash beloved books, music, and quality clothing, she had stuffed countless other reminders of her childhood into the confines of that minuscule space. Jennifer dragged out dusty diaries, youth group mementos, frayed sports ribbons, dog-eared yearbooks, and even sticky remnants of who-knew-how-old Easter candy!

At last, Jennifer had retrieved every abandoned article and dust bunny from her daughter's bed. Looking around, she realized that organizing all this stuff was going to take a significant time commitment. What's more, it would also require an emotional investment. Clutching Haley's worn-to-shreds-by-love stuffed dinosaur, Jennifer gulped. Cleaning was all well and good, but was she ready to take a stroll down memory lane in the process? And at such an emotionally volatile time? Tea, Jennifer decided. *A cup of fragrant, tasty tea always does me good.*

Basking in the late afternoon sunlight, Jennifer relaxed. Holding her favorite teacup in hand, she breathed in the delicate aroma of her tea of choice, citrus splendor. Spicy, yet smooth. As she sipped, she fell into a brief spell of melancholy. She knew this day would eventually arrive. Still, even with all her preparation, Jennifer—officially a newcomer to the ranks of empty nesters—wasn't all that sure she was prepared for the next step in her life's journey.

Sure, she'd been making all the appropriate plans for the day when Haley moved out of the house and left for an out-of-state college. Certainly, Jennifer had been diligent in facing this auspicious change. So why did her heart ache so? Why did it pain her to see all those mementos—all those memories of Haley's childhood—tossed glibly aside? *I know the answer, Jennifer* thought sadly. What mother wouldn't feel a vast expanse of nothingness when her child leaves home? *It makes sense. I hurt when I gave birth; it hurts to let go. Such is the stuff of life!*

The women who best acclimate to challenging situations or life-altering changes are those who are mentally and spiritually aware.

Closing her eyes, Jennifer prayed. *Lord, help me. Come swiftly to my aid as you have done so many times in the past. Always my faithful Lord, you know my every thought, my every fear. Calm me now, in these troublesome days when life as I know it is changing forever. Give me your grace to see this change as a gift from your hand. Let me not shirk from the unknown, but rather face each day, every moment, with full assurance that you will walk me through to the other side. Enable me to step positively into this brand new future. I trust in your strength, your goodness, and your love. Amen.*

With new resolve, Jennifer rinsed her cup, wiped the wet ring off the kitchen table, and determined to make some real progress yet that day in Haley's room. Making her way up the stairs, Jennifer's spirits flagged a bit, but then she remembered how she had faced so many other "adjustments" as a single mom. One step at a time. One small choice at a time.

All right now, maybe if I get this paper problem under control first, the rest will be simpler. After stacking pile upon pile of miscellaneous paper, Jennifer started sorting. Fifteen minutes became sixty, then ninety. When the room lost its luster from the sun's final rays, Jennifer got up, stretched, and went to turn on Haley's bedside lamp. Perched half under, half next to, its stand, Jennifer noticed some travel brochures. Pulling the top one out, Jennifer smiled as she read its contents. Each one detailed a different adventure trip; one to a dude ranch, another white water rafting, the third a mountain climbing excursion. That daredevil girl of mine! Always planning for her next venture.

Putting the pamphlets back in place, a sudden thought occurred to Jennifer. Why not? The parallel is certainly there. Maybe, just maybe, I'll ask Haley if she wouldn't mind some company. After all, life's to be an adventure, right?

Ready, Set, Adjust!

☼ *Forge new relationships apart from your children.* Renee woke up one day and suddenly realized that virtually every social contact she had was somehow connected to her son's social circle. The parents of the boys her son played with became Renee's friends by default; nothing wrong with that. After all we often choose friends based on common interests or, in this case, mutual friends. But Renee wondered what was going to happen once her son grew up. After her son outgrew his need for a chauffeur, would Renee's current cache of female friends continue to befriend her? Or were their friendships tied to their sons' relationships? Good question. Renee decided then and there to begin seeking out a few other women she was acquainted with and begin cultivating some social activity that was based on Renee as a person, independent of her offspring.

✸ *Invest time and energy in developing skills, abilities, and talents.* Being a mom takes the majority (and sometimes all) of a woman's concentration and daily energy. Thus, most moms have little "extra" to spare once they've fulfilled their basic responsibilities. Though it might feel awkward at first, midlife single moms who are reaching that transitional place between their kids' blossoming independence and the empty nest wisely take some well-spent hours simply to "introspect." They remember what they were good at, what they loved doing pre-mommyhood. These thoughtful women also revisit earlier life goals and then put in place opportunities to enhance their lives with valued and valuable activity.

✸ *Proactively step into life independent of the lives of your children.* Cathy sat in the parking lot of the ladies gym. She felt her palms moisten and wiped them on her thighs. I can't do this, Cathy thought . . . What's the matter with me? Answering her own silent query, Cathy recognized that it had been years since she had done anything significant apart from her kids' activities. Sure, she could handle whatever life threw her way when it came to parenting, but this was different. Suddenly, Cathy was attempting to step into a role where she was the focus of attention. Up to now, most of her life had centered on enabling her children to grow and succeed. Taking a deep breath, Cathy realized it was high time she experienced a bit of stretching for her own sake, and she wasn't thinking about how her muscles would ache come evening. I've got to do this . . . and she did do it but, Cathy conceded, the stretching came with some residual aches and pains.

✸ *Find the will and the courage to step into unknown territory.* When Sally's ex-husband left her during the early years of parenting, she was bereft in every possible way—financially, emotionally, spiritually. But Sally had a small group of friends who came alongside her, comforted her, listened to her complaints, and then cheered her on to better days. Some six years after her unwanted divorce, Sally graduated with a degree in business and now manages her own at-home health care enterprise. Sally often gives credit to those who believed in her ability to succeed when she didn't feel she had the strength even to get out of bed.

❀ *Ease emotionally into the empty nest by anticipating its arrival.* Taking a proactive approach to life is one of the primary ways to ensure smooth transitions and eventual success. The women who best acclimate to challenging situations or life-altering changes are those who are mentally and spiritually aware. These women are prepared, stand at the ready, and literally anticipate the ever-shifting phases of life. By adopting a faith-enthused, positive, can-do perspective, moms "can do" whatever it is that needs to be accomplished.

❀ *Stay prayerfully engaged while allowing your children room to grow up and leave.* When Ruth waved good-bye to her twin daughters, she cried buckets. Yet her weeping wasn't characterized by emotional devastation. Rather, thankfulness and a grateful spirit frequently marked Ruth's prayers. Ruth was fully confident that even though she wouldn't be able to speak words of encouragement to her girls daily, she could offer a greater gift. Ruth determined to invest her parental energy in interceding for her daughters from every vantage point. She realized that no one would ever pray for her girls as she would. So Ruth found quiet solace and sweet comfort in bringing every request, large and small, before Christ in prayer. She often got up from her knees wondering if she wasn't the one who was most blessed after such heavenly encounters.

❀ *Resolve to think and act positively toward all changes.* Jill was the mother of five children. All but one were grown and had left home. Jill looked back and marveled at the speed at which the mothering years had passed by. While her home is quieter these days, her heart and mind continue to relive those moments when God's presence and provision made all the difference. Certainly, Jill and her children had gone without many of the perks other families take for granted. But Jill realized God's hand had provided for their every need. So why fret the future? Already seasoned by years of God's faithfulness, Jill took time to give thanks every day. And she, like other great women of faith, was not afraid of tomorrow.

※ *Partner with other parents who have already walked the path.* Becky and Susan had been friends since elementary school. They had grown up together. Now, they were growing old(er) together as well. The only significant difference between them was that Becky was parenting a ten-year-old. Susan had married right after college while Becky had first pursued a career. While Susan's children were all grown and on their own, Becky was just entering the jumping off phase. Daily, sometimes hourly, Becky would make urgent 911 calls to Susan for small doses of emotional respite and perspective. Becky realized how precious Susan's counsel and comfort was . . . and how timely. She'd already walked this road. Who better to confer with?

Every Mother's Prayer

Lord,

I stand at the crossroads, often unsure and uncertain of the next step. I frequently find myself wondering if I've done all I could do as a mom. Have I passed on my faith, my values, everything that is of eternal worth? Will my children still hear and abide by those timeless truths even when they've moved on? My heart, I admit, is often marked by fearful thoughts. Lord, will you stand with me now? Please, be my guardian, my friend, and my counselor. I have such need of your wisdom, instruction, and grace. Grace! Oh how I long for a renewed measure of your sweet grace to see me through this time of change. Let my mind and my heart be fixed upon you and your good word. When I feel tempted to draw back in fear or pity, nudge me forward. Enable me to continue serving day by day, hour by hour, even though my life may continually change. Help me recount your faithfulness from days past. Remind me of who you are. And never let me neglect the privilege of prayerful intercession—for myself and for my children. Link me to your heart, and let not despair or discouragement tear me from your presence. As always, I depend on your strength and your mercy to continue my journey. Thank you, Lord, for loving me, for forgiving me, for redeeming me. Amen.

Thought for the Day

"In the Bible I find the Creator who made me and therefore knows everything about me. I find a Savior who walked on earth in my shoes and understands everything about my experience. The Bible faces the deepest issues of the human experience head-on, with bright hope and functional wisdom."

—*Lost in the Middle: Midlife and the Grace of God,* by Paul David Tripp

Chapter Two

Gathering Strength for the Last Hurrah

Endurance to Finish Strong

All Scripture is God-breathed and is useful for teaching, rebuking, correcting and training in righteousness, so that all God's people may be thoroughly equipped for every good work.
2 Timothy 3:16

There is a common thread amongst midlife moms whose sons and daughters are at that "jumping off" stage. It's called premature disengagement and it can be terminal—as deadly as any physical disease. And no, it isn't the kids who are prematurely disengaging, it is the moms. Surprised? Don't be. Disengagement happens in every home. The question is not *if* it will occur, but *how* will each woman handle it when she comes to that pivotal intersection?

Let's look at the typical disengagement scenario. To successfully disengage a mother eyes the problem, large or small, and within seconds makes a choice. Will she or won't she engage her heart, mind, and soul into the issue at hand? At this point in life, this midlife juncture, women see vistas opening up before them—a whole world out there for the taking. And they wonder, during those fleeting decision-making moments, whether or not they are going to re-invest themselves (yet again) in their family's problems.

It's so tempting to disengage; every woman has done it . . . quite successfully for that matter, and more times than we care to recall, if we are truly honest. When situations get too "icky" or too intense it is simpler and far less draining to walk away emotionally. And yet, moms continue to hear this voice in their heads that reminds them the job isn't complete. They have to finish what they started. (Isn't that what every mother has been telling her kids for years?)

Herein lies the rub. Will moms be honest enough to adhere to their own motherly counsel? Or will they opt out early and find more instantly satisfying gratification in their personal retreats? It is difficult, this choice. We mothers are always aware that time marches on and we are growing our kids "up" to move them "out," in the best sense of the word.

Still, on a moment-by-moment basis our worlds can shift. One moment our young adult children can themselves choose to retreat back into temporary parental dependency when life gets too demanding. Then we gently nudge them back out. The next moment they're telling us they can handle it (code for "back off"). This three-steps-forward, two-steps-backward dance is part of the maturing process. Often, we don't realize that this intentional growing up junket is just as difficult on us as it is on our young adult children. We feel a similar push/pull, rush/retreat reaction to life stresses in ways that mirror our kids' responses.

> *We mothers are always aware that time marches on and we are growing our kids "up" to move them "out," in the best sense of the word.*

They want out. We want them to be ready and prepared to face life, fully equipped for every eventuality. They try out their independence and it fits for the moment, the next it doesn't. This back and forth movement can render moms dizzy, off-kilter, and weary of trying to second-guess what their role is at any given minute. Moms sometimes wistfully wonder when it will be over, this intense mothering task that has required more of them than they ever thought they were able to give.

Maggie had just gotten up and wasn't quite fully awake when her son soberly informed her that her eighteen-year-old daughter's car had been vandalized during the night. Maggie stood there in the chilly kitchen trying to take in all the sordid details of the minor crime—the smashed bananas, the toilet paper, and worst of all, the graffiti written on her daughter's car windows. To add insult to injury, this occurred on Thanksgiving Day . . . or night rather . . . thus accentuating Maggie's feeling of being supremely violated. Which of my daughter's friends—and she used the term "friend" loosely—would feel comfortable writing such foul words in plain sight of the world and, more specifically, in our private driveway?

Maggie couldn't think clearly. She was so offended, and wondered when her daughter had begun associating with young men who clearly didn't comprehend the meaning of demonstrating respect for women. A myriad of conflicting thoughts and emotions passed like a freight train through her mind. Some of them Maggie was ashamed to confess, of the reprisal sort.

As the mother of three young adult daughters and a teenage son, Maggie took her parenting task to heart—always had. She had spent the better part of the last twenty-plus years investing in the physical, emotional, and spiritual well-being of her offspring, not to mention her efforts to impart to each of them the value of a life characterized by integrity and a mind cognizant of the needs of those around them. She now guessed this term "selflessness" has gone out of vogue. Still, it's a message they needed to hear . . . and internalize.

So, standing in her kitchen on that blustery post-holiday morning, Maggie was in part upset with the situation (that outside forces beyond her control were trespassing on this single mom's idea of a gentler, more thoughtful private world) and in part frustrated with her own reaction. Since her children were no longer "kids" Maggie had noticed she was slowly but progressively finding herself investing more of herself in her work, her friends, and other formerly impractical avocations. This, Maggie found, was good. The negative side to her creative rebirth is that she too often retreated to these areas of life where she felt comfortable in her own performance . . . where the pain associated with parenting and the whole letting go issue didn't touch her, or her heart. Maggie had to decide what to do on this particular day with this specific problem. Engage or not?

Perhaps then, Maggie's reaction to her daughter's car being ravaged had more to do with her realization that she had precious little time left to invest in her children's lives, that her illusion of control (the feeling that kept her feeling safe) had just about evaporated. Maggie realized, yet again, that she couldn't control what happens outside the four walls of her home. Often, she felt unable even to offer a safe retreat inside it. And it truly is a dangerous, harsh world out there. All these thoughts and more rushed through Maggie's mind.

Today's opportunity to impact your child's life will never again present itself in quite the same way, so make the most of every occasion to offer guidance.

So what's a mom to do? she wondered. Shrugging in silent resignation, Maggie realized she'd already decided. She would stay with the task of parenting until (A) there was no one left to listen to her mother them into acts of kindness and/or responsible living, or (B) she could see by their lives that they had been paying attention and were yielding the positive, life-affirming fruits they'd been spoon fed for the past twenty years. Maggie smiled ruefully, realizing her kids still needed her input, and her actively engaged emotional, mental, and spiritual investment in their lives. Possibly they always would.

In now somewhat happy resignation, Maggie reasoned silently, I think I'll know when it's time to stop. I'm just not there yet.

Ready, Set, Adjust!

View life from a seasonal perspective. Today's opportunity to impact your child's life will never again present itself in quite the same way, so make the most of every occasion to offer guidance. Lisa felt worn thin by her tiring day at the real estate office. All afternoon she kept envisioning a simple dinner, doing a few loads of laundry, and then unplugging with a good book. What Lisa got was a surprise request to go on a bike ride around the neighborhood with her daughter Chris. Tempted to decline because of exhaustion, Lisa stopped herself and said yes before giving it a second thought. I can forgo the reading for an hour, Lisa thought. How often does one of my own kids come to me with the opportunity to go riding with them anymore? And just maybe Chris wants to toss around her newest ideas for moving next spring.

Resist the "only if I have something tangible to show for my efforts" mentality when responding to your children. Remember that investing in people always pays the highest dividends. Amy was a seasoned and successful businesswoman. After years of sacrifice, she now managed her city's top human resources company. She has this instinctive gift for reading people accurately and matching recruits with employers. At day's end, nothing is more satisfying to Amy than revisiting how many new placements she has orchestrated. So why was it seemingly impossible for her to offer the same "investment" in time toward her son Evan? It was unlike her to be so lackadaisical. And yet, Amy realized that rarely did she ever see any progress or "returns" from her conversations with Evan. As a woman of faith, Amy knew better than to live solely by what her eyes tell her. Convicted and resolved, in typical can-do Amy fashion, she decided that tonight she would start afresh with Evan. Before he even arrived home, she would "invest" herself in her son's life by praying diligently and daily for him. He doesn't even have to know, Amy thought. This is a mother's gift to her only son.

✺ *Stop the wearisome "not this again" mindset before it can take hold and rob you of the opportunity to find new ways to solve old problems.* Martha stopped herself from "going there" in her mind. As she perused the daily mail, opening the bank statements had been a mistake. She saw that now. Too late. Another overdraft charge had been applied to her youngest daughter's checking account. When? When? When is Amanda going to start listening to me when it comes to handling her money? I have tried and tried to get through to her. A person cannot spend money they do not have. A sale is not a good deal if you do not have the cash to pay for it. And what happens if her car breaks down? What then? Stop it! Martha suddenly realized that rehashing this internal litany was getting her nowhere fast. Inhaling deeply, she decided to enlist the support of another mom who has been through a similar situation. She made a call to a good friend whose kids are now grown and gone, one of whom, Martha recalled, had given his mom financial fits. She felt better already, just knowing there was someone to call for a pep talk and fresh advice. Don't get stuck in the quicksand of the "not this again" mentality. Approach familial issues with the same acumen and fresh energy you extend to business or professional endeavors. Keep looking for new ways to address and dismantle old stumbling blocks.

✺ *Bank on past successes as the foundation to endure present challenges; don't waste life today by borrowing on tomorrow's uncertainties.* Emily is an expert rememberer. She has to be. With four college-aged teens continually swooping in and out of her house, Emily never has the time or the luxury to forget how God has met her needs and those of the kids over the years. As a suddenly widowed single mom, Emily had had to sell their sprawling country home and move closer to town and into a house with a smaller mortgage. Emily revisited those early years and the tough financial adjustments and sacrifices they all made together. Looking back, it was hard. And yet, Emily saw God provide and her kids' faith grow stronger, their family unit knit tighter. Today, when another college tuition bill arrives, Emily gets excited . . . well, almost . . . for she knows without a doubt that it is God's faithfulness alone that brought them to a place where college for her four kids was even a remote possibility.

☀ *Expect young adults to vacillate between moving out and stepping back. Expect to encounter some emotional distress as they work through the push/pull stretch for independence.* Dianna feels like tearing her hair out. One day her daughter and best friend are moving into an apartment, the next they want to "redecorate" the garage dormer and live there. Indecision. Dianna wonders if she was ever that indecisive. Ever. It is driving her crazy. Either choice has its pros and cons and Dianna has dutifully pointed each one out to her daughter. But instead of receiving a "Thanks Mom," Dianna was met with an exasperated sigh and a not-so-subtle hint to leave them be. That's fine, Dianna thought, I'll be the role model for hands-off parenting on this one. I just wish my daughter had some type of external signal for me to know when I'm "allowed" to offer my suggestions.

☀ *See yourself as the team leader and coach whose sole desire is to equip and train participants to be successful winners in any endeavor they undertake.* Beth and her daughter Katherine have always had a close, tender relationship. Until D-day. When boyfriend Dustin entered the picture, Katherine changed completely. No longer did she look to Beth for guidance. It was Dustin this and Dustin that, until Beth could hardly stomach it any longer. If Dustin's advice were sound,

Beth would be fine with this replacement counselor. But the truth is, Dustin's ideas were never, ever, sensible—and Beth was being generous in her assessment. Finally, after Dustin recommended to a starry-eyed Katherine that she drop out of school at mid term because she isn't happy with her professors, Beth text messaged her daughter and set up a lunch date. Beth has been praying that she will be able to communicate in a way that will help Katherine listen and reopen the doors of counsel that have been shut tight. Food and a festive atmosphere, Beth hopes, might soften the way for her to challenge Katherine's current decisions and rethink to whom she goes for advice.

☀ *Find ways to respectfully and effectively communicate the on/off angst response you're experiencing as a mother who's torn between yesterday's intensive childrearing years and today's tenuous, ever-altering parenting position.* Sharon was beside herself. From one conversation to the next, her sons either shunned her or they embraced her with rib-splitting bear hugs. Mark, her oldest, is the most unpredictable and Sharon decided they needed to update the "house rules" before she grows any more bruised, emotionally or otherwise. One evening after dinner, Sharon sat her boys down for a brief but straight-to-the-point family meeting. Her goal? Cut Mom some slack and always, always offer a respectful response, even when in disagreement. Sharon no longer accepts her sons' cavalier—and at times condescending—retorts that leave her feeling like she has done something wrong. The three of them will work hard to see that their family dynamics change and that grace becomes the new byword for the way they live and speak. No negotiations up for discussion on this one.

☀ *Remember that oft-bestowed motherly advice: a job isn't done until it's done. Stay with the parenting task until it's complete.* Parenting is a God-ordained, God-enabled responsibility. In all truth, moms don't have the choice to decide when to stop "mothering" for they are under a higher authority and accountable to God for their actions. Ellen told her son and daughter over and over again to finish one job before they begin another. Keep life simple. Don't put too many irons in the fire at once or everything will get burned. Then, after one exasperatingly harried weekend of her own, Ellen realized she hadn't been taking her own advice. Paring back on her commitments, even the slightest bit, afforded Ellen not only more flex time, but more family time.

Every Mother's Prayer

Lord,

I'm here at this specific time and place to be an influence, a guide, and a support for my children. Help me not to give up before my parenting task is done. So often I stand wondering what my role is as a mother to my almost-grown children. I find myself offering my opinions, my thoughts, and my counsel without hesitation. Then I realize my kids aren't always so ready to hear me as they did when they were young. And maybe it would be better for them and for me if I keep silent more often and allow them to try their hand at working through the day's problems and challenges. Seems like I have my own share of obstacles and more often than not, I'm concentrating on handling MY life. I admit that of late I've been sorely tempted to let my children go off on their own too often and too soon. I'm simply weary of the struggles, the difficulties in communicating, and my energy level is pretty well depleted. Frequently, the cry of my heart is: Enough! This is why I so need your hand of strength, your faithful encouragement, and your eternal perspective to be persistent in offering the love and grace you want me to impart to these children of mine. I have only one opportunity to be their mother. Let me continue to parent well and wisely until my job is truly complete. Amen.

Thought for the Day

"A parent who has his hope in the Gospel will pursue his teenagers and will not stop until they leave the home. We won't wait for them to come to us for help. We won't argue with them as to whether we are needed or not. The call of the Word is clear. With hearts filled with Gospel hope, we will question and probe, listen and consider, plead and encourage, admonish and warn, and instruct and pray. We will awake every day with a sense of mission, knowing that God has given us a high calling."

—*Age of Opportunity: A Biblical Guide to Parenting Teens,* by Paul David Tripp

Chapter Three

Imparting Vision and Setting Goals

Foundations for Making Wise Choices

> *If any of you lacks wisdom, you should ask God, who gives generously to all without finding fault, and it will be given to you.*
> James 1:5

Where are you heading? Do you know? Have you made plans for the upcoming years? The next twelve months? This week? Today? These are important questions that deserve adequate time and attention. In his book *The Search for Satisfaction*, author David McKinley reminds us that "Whenever you exit planet Earth, your grave will bear a marker of time—a tombstone or memorial plaque. What is found on most? The dates of your birth and death. Life is what happens in the 'dash' between the two" (35).

If you know where you're heading, you'll be of much greater help to your offspring as they navigate the murky waters of post-high school educational and career choices. No matter what our age, moms and kids alike make decisions every single day. And yes, it takes courage to risk entering new and untested territory. But that's just another facet of mothering, isn't it? That innate ability to "hand off" the baton of confidence to our teens and young adult children is instinctive to motherhood. While moms cannot always tell their children how to determine which course to take with 100 percent accuracy, they can help them develop sound decision-making criteria and critical thinking skills to better equip them. In short, moms impart the "know-how" so that their young adult kids know how to address pivotal and ongoing life choices.

If you know where you're heading, you'll be of much greater help to your offspring as they navigate the murky waters of post-high school educational and career choices.

From experience, moms also recognize that lacking "on paper" goals, those passing "pipe dreams" frequently die a quick death at the first sign of opposition or the slightest, most incidental setback. Everyone knows someone whose dreams are routinely larger than life. These individuals are colorfully over the top with excitement and enthusiasm, and are enthralled with the *idea* of some far-removed notion of success. While it's fun (and amusing) to watch such theatrics, if we're honest we're pretty certain very little by way of actual results will ever come to pass. We've borne witness to the same song and dance too many times before and while we resist reacting with a sort of subdued, mild cynicism, it isn't always easy to join in with the fleeting momentary hilarity either. There's just too much to lose.

Mothers want to inspire their kids to dream big, while simultaneously equipping them with practical ways to reach these same objectives. Look at history (both the grand and the small) for a more tempered response to "dreaming." Clearly, it is those individuals (and nations) who take careful account of their gifts, talents, abilities, resources, and limitations that most often achieve their intents. Sure, there are setbacks, risks, and sacrifices. But for people who know their destination, these wrinkles can be ironed out and smoothed over because the end goal (written in black and white, remember) is an ever-present reminder of what is at stake. Writer David McKinley believes that, "Life reflects design, sequence, and order" (*Search for*

Satisfaction, 34). Thus, finding practical ways to work toward our target means settling down with one hand firmly grasped on reality while balancing the most hopeful possibilities etched in our brain on the other. McKinley asks, "Are you living 'on purpose,' or have you given your life over to the random acts of occurrence—wishing, hoping, and yearning?" (37). Good question for every mom to ask, first of herself, and then model to her children.

After listening to her son Nick's phone message that he was on his way home, Karen was tempted to plop down on the couch and have a full-blown pity party. She deserved it. At least, that's what she kept telling herself. Throwing good money after bad. Wasn't that the old saying her own mother used to repeat whenever the family discussed loaning money to her notorious Uncle Bill, the one and only person in the Baker clan who never held a job longer than six months? The one and only uncle who didn't keep a current home address simply because he never stayed in one city long enough for the mail to catch up with him. The one and only uncle no one respected or had much use for.

Karen shook her head in dismay. I finally get it. Now I understand what my mom meant when she would shake her head in frustration over her brother's latest scheme to make money fast—for the most part without working for it. What did Mom say about Uncle Bill? He was aimless . . . that's it . . . an aimless wanderer . . . and his family often paid the price for his lack of stick-to-itiveness, his unwillingness to stay with a plan long enough to recoup his (or the family's) investment. Karen believed her mom—shortcuts don't work, never have, and never will.

Finding practical ways to work toward our target means settling down with one hand firmly grasped on reality while balancing the most hopeful possibilities etched in our brain on the other.

Eyes squeezed in consternation, Karen wryly wondered how large a part genetics played into her son Nick's current mirroring of Uncle Bill's antics. Recoiling from the imaginary mental image of the two of them side by side panhandling their lives away, Karen prayed mightily against any unseen spiritual foes that might influence her son, or even tempt him, to give way to the path of least resistance and, worse yet, be content to do so.

As Karen continued to rehearse the four years since Nick's graduation from high school, her emotions vacillated in tandem with the highs and lows of each memory. Some were precious, others not so endearing. How pleased and proud Karen had been when Nick received a full scholarship to their hometown university. Always the avid reader and late night bookworm, Nick had taken to his studies like there was no tomorrow. Graduating near the top of his class, with honors and advanced placement tests soaring, Karen had entertained high hopes for her oldest son. Never, ever did she anticipate having to "coach" and cajole Nick into finishing out semester after semester at college. Karen couldn't recall ever having to press Nick to complete any of his high school requirements, and many of them were demanding, intense, and extremely rigorous. What had triggered this sudden lack of direction and responsibility? Karen still didn't understand it.

So her mind raced over the troubling and financially incapacitating scenario again and again. It all began with Nick switching to an "undecided" major within weeks of his first freshman semester, and then things seemed to skid downhill from there, into the infuriating habit (for Karen) of enrolling/dropping/reenrolling season by season—Karen just about went crazy with worry. Eventually, Nick didn't even meet the minimum requirements for maintaining his scholarship. So he lost it. All that money—gone. It hurt Karen's heart just to think about it. And what had been Nick's glib response? "I'll take out loans." And he did. Against her better judgment and her counsel, Nick plowed ahead, certain he knew better than his mom. Karen wished this one time Nick had been right. But he wasn't.

Instead of buckling down now that college tuition was no longer free, Nick continued to dabble on the surface of one discipline after another. Until last spring, that is, when he let slip he had not been attending school at all for several months. Nick decided it was a waste of time for him to attend college without knowing what he wanted to do with his life. Silently praying for grace to restrain her rising anger, Karen was almost afraid to ask Nick what his current plans were. But she needn't have been concerned—Nick just came out with it. He was going to earn enough cash working the night shift at a nearby bakery to cover traveling funds to Europe for the summer with some buddies from college. Of course, his friends were going overseas and earning credit for it. Nick was just . . . going. No plan. No worries. No ideas about narrowing down his career options. No thought of paying back his loan six months from the date he dropped out.

Suddenly Karen couldn't breathe. It was physically impossible to take even one deep, cleansing breath. With her heart racing and her chest tightening painfully, Karen wanted to scream some sense into Nick. Problem was, she couldn't take a breath deep enough to utter a whisper let alone shout at the boy. Rising to her feet and getting away from her son helped calm Karen. Within a few minutes the panic passed. Well, the panic attack passed. Karen recognized she still had loads of parenting work ahead of her. That memorable afternoon was only the beginning of a string of angry, convoluted conversations she endured with Nick over his future.

But today would go down in Karen's family history as the day she changed her tactics and her focus with her son. With list in hand, Karen had prayed over and through this troubling, never-ending debacle, and it was going to stop today. Nick might not honor all her wishes, but he was going to hear Karen out, or . . . he'll be moving out. While Nick didn't need to be treated like a child, it was clear to Karen he still required enough direction and boundaries to get his life back on track with some solid intervention guidelines. Karen decided it wasn't healthy for her or her son to continue the way they had been living—Karen in constant angst, Nick oblivious to reality.

She also realized it was going to take courage to take a stand and get both of them going in a new direction. Push has come to shove, Karen realized. I think I'm finally ready. Nick's not going to do this on his own apparently. And I'm certainly not bankrolling his irresponsibility, Karen thought. If Nick wants to play at life, then he can do it on his own dime and under another roof.

Ready, Set, Adjust!

※ *Make a five year plan, dream big, but set the goal on paper for continued reflection, and do not be hesitant to tweak the plan . . . expect to do so.* Barb was so organized her kids often teased her about having her funeral date scheduled in advance. Truth was, Barb wasn't born with a special giant-sized organizational gene. She had, however, been the youngest in a large boisterous family of six children in a home where chaos reigned supreme. Barb, quiet by nature, often felt lost in the shuffle of the family's noisy commotion. There were times when she was literally left behind, forgotten both at home and during family getaways. Now, as the head of her own family, Barb decided early on to set ideas, plans, and goals on paper and on the calendar. She also relies on automatic computer prompts that appear across her screen in regular succession. The kids might poke fun, Barb thought, but they'll thank me someday when they realize how putting schedules and goals down in black and white simplifies and streamlines a person's life.

※ *Accurately assess present "pluses," which includes all personal (and financial) abilities, skills, talents, education, and experience.* Optimistic that her daughter was going to attend the family college, Rachel just couldn't get over the disappointment that Taylor had no interest in adding to the family's prestigious legacy. In fact, Taylor wasn't interested in attending college period. She opted for a trade school where she would become qualified as a dental assistant within two years. Degrees with letters before or after her name simply didn't matter to Taylor, but she found great satisfaction in working with people and was a real hands-on kind of person. After some private stewing and foot stamping, Rachel realized that Taylor is simply different from her. Not less, just unlike her. After feeling convicted of trying to live out some of her own dreams through her daughter's life, Rachel made a dramatic U-turn in her attitude and became Taylor's number one supporter and confidante. It became a win-win situation for both of them.

☀ *Be realistic about limitations, including past shortfalls and mistakes, and pay close attention to situations that are most difficult or challenging.* Chelsea watched and waited, certain that her daughter Katie would "make good" at her newest job at the upscale shopping mall. But it wasn't to be. Katie just got flustered and upset (bringing those frustrations home with her nightly) when she had to wait on demanding customers who cut her no slack if she made an error or wasn't able to respond instantly to their inquires. Katie had never been good at thinking on her feet or under pressure. But she had other strengths . . . lots of them. Though Chelsea's mother's heart just about broke each time Katie came home feeling like a perpetual misfit at work, Chelsea realized that Katie needed to reassess her skills and abilities. Maybe the reason Katie continued to "fail" was that she kept placing herself in the same situation. Might be a different store, a different job title, but Katie continued to choose those positions that drew attention to her weaknesses instead of playing on her strengths.

☀ *Ask for input from others who are where you want to be and invite the counsel of trusted friends, family, and colleagues on a regular basis.* Mary and Rebekah had been best friends since childhood. Different as they were, the two used each other as sounding boards before either of them made crucial life decisions. With their monthly coffee date approaching, Mary made a note to ask Rebekah how and why she had steered her sons into the military rather than college. With her own son tossing around the idea of signing up for the armed forces, Mary felt afraid and daunted by the commitment. Though his college tuition would be covered, was it worth the risk? Mary wrote down all her questions and decided to leave the issue alone until she could discuss the matter with Rebekah in person. Just the thought of good counsel with a great cup of coffee laced with cream made Mary relax.

❄ *Do the necessary research, stay current, and keep the overall plan in the forefront of your mind while attending to the small daily steps in between.* Lynn was busy working on her back-to-school agenda for the fall. After years of being an at-home single mom, her kids are now out of the house and Lynn is ready to complete that final year of college she never finished when she got pregnant with her first child all those long years ago. Excited and somewhat daunted, Lynn sat thinking about how she "coached" her three kids through high school and then college. All those nights when they wanted to give up, Lynn told them to hang tough, keep at it, and they would never regret their investment. Sighing, Lynn asked the Lord to give her the same "talking to" when she would want to give up on her dream of finishing her degree. She knew she is no different from her kids, there would be days, maybe even weeks, when she would ask herself if the cost was worth it. "Small successes," isn't that what Lynn had told her kids to find comfort and solace in? Focus on the final goal, but be encouraged by every single step you take along the way.

❄ *Never give up. Expect opposition; don't run from it. Instead, adopt a student mentality; be ready to learn from every situation.* Twenty-one-year-old Jillian cried all the way home. She had flunked chemistry again, for the third time. She was so upset, so embarrassed. Her older sister never had this problem. Kelly had breezed through her science and math courses. So why do I have so much trouble? Before Jillian could even utter a word, she heard her mom's admonition to get a tutor . . . but she hadn't listened. Jillian didn't think she needed one, oops. The hardest part to stomach was that her mom warned her that she herself would have to pay for the course if she didn't pass because she didn't get outside help. What was I thinking, Jillian steamed, and why didn't I listen? I know what Mom will say, "Don't give up, but be smarter this time and ask for help from the start."

※ *Be flexible and open to changing direction when warranted.* Three years into the elementary education program, Joe decided he didn't want to teach the rest of his life. He didn't even know if he liked kids. Well, that was an epiphany! Joe thought and thought about how to break the news to his schoolteacher mom. Well, no time like the present. Better today than after graduation, right? Or after working a few years and hating it. I sure wouldn't be doing any favors to my prospective students if I despised being there, would I?

※ *Communicate with care and respect when offering experience or advice.* Stephanie loves her daughter Megan and the two are as close as can be. Problem is, Stephanie recognizes that Megan is her mirror image. This is both good and bad. When the conversation shifts to touchy subjects, the temperature rises between the two of them, neither of whom is very skilled at backing down. Since Stephanie is the mom, it's her responsibility to take the lead in setting both the tone and content of their conversations, otherwise Megan's ears won't be open to hearing what she has to hear and they both end up angry and frustrated.

Every Mother's Prayer

Lord,

True enough, there were times when it felt like I was the one doing all the learning while my kids lived oblivious to the real seriousness of the situation. Oh, how afraid I was in those times, second-guessing my choices and my ability to provide what they needed. Still, as I listened and learned, and leaned in and trusted, You cared and directed our every step. So now, I come before You asking that once again You give wisdom, understanding, and discernment to my family and me. Each of us is at a decision-making juncture. I pray that You impart the necessary decision-making skills to choose wisely in the upcoming days and weeks. Help us determine, by diligent prayer and careful planning, what course You have laid before us. Help us to be courageous enough to step out in faith, confident in Your sustaining power and strength. We want our lives to be full and effective for Your glory. We want our love for others to be evident in all we undertake, all the days of our lives. Lord, place Your good hand of care and guidance upon us and lead us on. We gladly wait for You to shepherd us along life's pathway, knowing full well that in You alone is safety and certainty. Amen.

Thought for the Day

"When God calls people to do something, their initial response is almost always fear. If there is a challenge in front of you, a course of action that could cause you to grow and that would be helpful to people around you, but you find yourself scared about it, there's a real good chance that God is in that challenge."

—*When the Game is Over: It All Goes Back in the Box,* by John Ortberg

Chapter Four

Navigating New Relational Territories

Wise Counsel for Marriage Preparation

*Therefore, as God's chosen people, holy and
dearly loved, clothe yourselves with compassion,
kindness, humility, gentleness and patience. . . .
And over all these virtues put on love, which
binds them all together in perfect unity.*
Colossians 3:12, 14

In his book *Sacred Influence*, author Gary Thomas writes, "Hope is not a strategy" (35). While Thomas' text specifically exhorts women to be proactive and bold within the confines of their marital relationships, he offers a principle that is relevant to all believers: regardless of our social circumstance, inaction is by far riskier than action.

In relational terms, respect, trust, selflessness—the giving and the receiving of it—are all keys to longevity and success. It doesn't matter whether we're talking about personal or workplace encounters, everyone appreciates and responds more positively if they're being treated with courtesy and dignity. If women want to have high-quality, mutually satisfying interchanges with others, then we have to make deliberate choices and be willing to persevere over the long haul. Says Thomas, "Endeavors require deliberate choices and much perseverance" (35).

This is never more true than in the preparation and the realizing of a God-honoring, personally fulfilling marriage relationship. Moms can "hope" all they want that their children will have great marriages, but without adequate and wise preparation all the hoping in the world won't ready sons and daughters for such a demanding lifelong commitment.

Nothing in life happens by accident. We mothers can attest to having had to rise above today's heartache while eyeing an uncertain future as we shore up our shaky selves with faith-driven hope. Even then, moms who have weathered severe marital distress and disappointment often feel their futures will, at best, resemble "patchworked" pieces sewn through their brokenness. Don't we want better for our children? For just as we instruct our children in the way of seeing further than today's temporary material gratification, so we must adopt a similarly far-reaching attitude in all our relationships (present and future); this includes both the planning and the realization of them. The question is, are we moms too busy, so distracted, that we forfeit our influence in helping prepare our offspring in practical ways for choosing wisely and rightly? Or is it simply too painful to revisit our own past?

We mothers can attest to having had to rise above today's heartache while eyeing an uncertain future as we shore up our shaky selves with faith-driven hope.

Mothers would do well to remember that forward thinking is the key to successful interpersonal relationships. We can never assume or bank on past experiences. Our kids won't learn from our mistakes by osmosis. Today is the only time we have to invest and effect a positive outcome. What we believe, say, and do today for our kids impacts all our tomorrows (theirs and our own). Preparation is essential. Mental and practical preparedness can make or break the trajectory of every relationship. We moms know this. Our task is to communicate these principles to the next generation.

So what's a mom to do? Do nothing by accident. Instead, ask yourself if you've given enough timely communication to fully prepare your children for making wise relational and marriage decisions. If not, remedy the error before the cost is too great.

Cindy rubbed her ring finger and wondered why, after all these years, her left hand still holds that familiar groove where her wedding and engagement rings once fit so snugly. It's comforting in a strange sort of way; that even though her husband Jeff is gone now, there remains a part of her that still bears witness to their failed marriage. One of the many ironies of life, she reflects, is that such a painful experience can also be the impetus that transforms life so powerfully.

Sitting on the back porch, Cindy surveyed her life. Marriage at a young age. (Because we were so in love.) Three kids within the first six years. (Major life adjustment.) Followed by a brief season of agreed-upon peace between her and Jeff while the children were in school. (Before the divorce fallout.)

Then her second life began, her after-the-divorce life. Her life as a single mom, a single-again woman, a woman whose heart was broken, but more importantly one whose life had been reshaped and renewed and restored. Amen, Cindy thought with intense gratefulness. It isn't often that she lingers long enough on the past to give it even a passing glance. But today is different. Today it is important to look back . . . and remember. Imperative even.

Today her daughter Gillian became engaged. Gulp. Even though Cindy saw it coming, probably well before Gillian herself did, it didn't make the event a bit easier to swallow. All these long years of parenting solo, Cindy had prayed and subtly hinted . . . well, maybe not so subtly . . . that her kids would do well to wait until their late twenties (at minimum) to marry, or even consider marriage. But did they listen? Nope. Here is Gillian, Cindy's eldest daughter, still a baby at twenty-one, getting married. Gillian. Married. For the life of her, Cindy can't even choke out the two words in a single sentence. What's the matter with me? Cindy groused. I should be

happy, ecstatic even. I love my daughter and I love Seth too. I do.
I mean, I really do, deep down in my heart of hearts, I love this
young man like he is my own.

And yet. What? Cindy just doesn't want to "go there." Not today.
Not on the single most important day in her daughter's life. Oh
why can't the past stay in the background, hidden away, discarded,
left untouched? Cindy tosses back her head and wants to scream
at the heavens. Instead, she breathes . . . deep. Exhales. Breathes
again, slower this time, and resignedly. Lord, you know what this
is going to cost me. And I know I have to work through the pain
of it. Huffing out a silent complaint, Cindy gives up. Gives in. She
knows what the Lord expects of her; there have been hints of it for
the last several years.

But Cindy was a master at evasion. It was a survival skill she'd
learned early on in her marriage to Jeff. When the pain grew to
mountainous proportions Cindy exited the scene, mentally that is.
She vacated the premises. Went AWOL. She was gone. No one could
blame her, could they? No one ever did. Who else would have put
up with Jeff's antics as long as she had? Precious few, if any. And
the truth was, every time Cindy attempted to stay engaged long
enough in conversation with Jeff to try and work out their latest
dispute, it always got twisted around. Was always her fault. Now,
that wasn't fair. In her heart, Cindy "got it" that life is rarely fair.
Still, when one's marriage was so up-ended toward the other spouse,
it felt intolerable. Inexcusable. And then there was the philandering.
Her fault too, of course. Sigh.

Okay, you win, Lord. At the risk of my sanity, I will do this. I
will think and pray and remember. I will, to the best of my ability,
call to mind exactly what transpired between Jeff and me. What
we did wrong and what we did right. I know that somewhere in
the midst of all that chaos and fighting and betrayal, we did start
out believing our marriage would make it over the long haul. Both
of us truly believed we understood what being joined together involved. In that, Jeff and I were on the same page at the beginning.
Even though our relationship soured fast, I can honestly offer my

Gillian a few nuggets of wisdom from my own experience. There were some slender golden moments amidst all the pain.

What hurt most, Cindy whispered to herself, was feeling that things would never change. Never heal. I grew embittered and spewed out in like quantity the very same poison Jeff sent my way, she admitted. Even though I was right, things didn't change. Even though I felt justified in expressing my outrageous anger, I was the one who changed. For the worse. How long did I allow Jeff's unfaithfulness and betrayal to cloud, color, and infect my whole world? she reflects.

Even after he vacated our house, our lives, I made him pay. With every thought of getting even, I never realized I was inflicting a worse punishment on myself. Such irony. What a shortsighted, costly blunder. If there is one lesson I can and need to teach my Gillian, it's that no matter how your life or your marriage plays out, you're still responsible for your own choices, your own responses, your own actions. Just knowing that, and making that single truth a reality, is what eventually set me free, Cindy thought. I only wish someone had come alongside me sooner and challenged me to muster the courage to move forward by forgiving Jeff early on.

Ask yourself if you've given enough timely communication to fully prepare your children for making wise relational and marriage decisions.

But the past is past. Eventually I did offer forgiveness, even though Jeff never saw a reason for me to express that to him. I did it anyway and that's what counts. And in the "doing," I was set free. So, I suppose there is a lesson even in that.

Lord, you promised to "restore the years the locusts have eaten," and so I ask you to teach me how to share what I've learned about marriage with those you've placed in my care, and to do so with a hopeful, faith-driven spirit. Amen.

Ready, Set, Adjust!

Re-evaluate your own marriage honestly and let your children benefit from your experience. What worked and what didn't? And why? Reflect back and write down on paper your thoughts about any missteps you took or things you would change if you could. Then note, given what you now know, what would have been the wisest choices; be ready to share these insights with your own children. Morgan mistakenly believed that if she hushed up all her former marriage problems with her ex-husband, her kids would be better off today. But what Morgan didn't realize—that is, until her college-aged son and daughter began mirroring the same poor communication practices of peace at any price or punishing with the silent treatment she and her ex-husband had acted out in front of them—is that her kids didn't have to be taught to handle conflict poorly. What they did need to learn is how to work through tough issues from a practical, biblical standpoint.

Assist children in laying biblical ground rules for all potentially romantic relationships. These rules should include principles such as being "equally yoked" and being spiritually mature enough to fully understand what each one's respective marriage role involves from a biblical perspective and the way these play out in everyday life. Laura had developed a system after her eldest son threw her a curveball when he told her he wanted to date a girl from school who didn't share his faith. Naturally, Laura sat Ian down and they talked specifics. Was Laura ever thankful she took the time to discuss the matter with Ian before giving him blanket permission. What Laura learned was disturbing; the girl in question not only didn't share Ian's budding faith, she was an outspoken atheist! So, what might have been a brief chat on where to go for dinner or what movie to see ended up being a lengthy discussion about developing basic dating guidelines based on matters of faith and other basic life principles.

※ *Teach young adults how to use the Bible as their foundation for marriage and their source of parenting models.* Do your children clearly understand basic principles for a Christian home based on scriptures that clearly provide instruction on leadership, submission, servanthood, finances, and goal setting? When Lisa first met her daughter's boyfriend from college, she liked him right off. But as time went on, red flags began to go up in Lisa's mind as she watched her daughter and boyfriend interact. Time and again, her daughter would repeat conversations where she was basically disagreeing and disrespecting her boyfriend and his decisions simply to make a point. After several months of hearing this repeated and disappointing refrain, Lisa decided to confront her daughter. Lisa questioned if her daughter would ever be willing to allow her boyfriend to lead in a marriage relationship if she was unable (unwilling) to recognize that God-ordained responsibility in him now?

※ *Ask your child if he or she is ready to work hard and is willing to sacrifice in order for the marriage to succeed.* Geoff and Leah sure had fun together. Everyone commented on how well they suited one another's penchant for extreme sports and other outdoor activities. But Geoff's mom, Tina, wondered if either of them understood that marriage often means going without the fun for days—even weeks—on end. That more sobering responsibility and faithfulness would quickly outweigh the more fickle emotions the two have experienced thus far as fellow pleasure seekers.

※ *Find out how your child views him- or herself.* Does she or he see her- or himself as a person in her or his own right, who is bringing something to the marriage, or is she or he looking to get their identity from their future spouse? Kelly couldn't relate to her daughter's constant "need" for a boyfriend. Ever since she had been a middle schooler, Joy wanted (and usually found) a willing young man to be her steady boyfriend. Kelly hoped she would outgrow this tendency as she grew up; but it had only become more intense, more pronounced. This weekend, Kelly decided, she and Joy will sit down and talk about where this desperate neediness comes from, and how to dismantle it.

☀ *Problem solve with your child by posing various typical and recurrent common struggles in marriage, and ask how he or she would go about working through each situation.* Dana decided her two girls were going to be as prepared for marriage as possible. So every Thursday evening, during an order-out pizza-fest and a chocolate almond fudge ice cream splurge, Dana and her daughters role-played every marriage scenario they could imagine. They loved it. Not only did Dana learn a lot about her daughters (their strengths and their weaknesses), they frequently ended up in laughing fits. The good humor lasted for days.

☀ *Discover your child's overall plan for financial management. Assist young adults in setting up a budget and financial goals for the long term.* Holly was an accountant; no doubt her sons and daughter would follow her expert budgeting model once they saw how quickly a dollar disappears. Not the case. Holly was beside herself, with an ex-spouse who spent, spent, spent, driving them into bankruptcy. Holly's mission in life was to educate her children before they slipped into the black hole of credit card debt. Maybe what they needed to see, Holly decided, is what we went through in black and "red" way back when. Perhaps then the kids will take my words to heart.

☀ *Together, study what the Scriptures have to say about marriage, divorce, and remarriage, underscoring that for Christian believers the marriage covenant is not one to be lightly discarded.* As Carol listened to her voice messages she felt her heart would break. She couldn't believe that her son was getting a divorce, even initiating one. This news blindsided her and brought back too many memories of her own broken marriage. Carol realized, too late, that she had not taken the time to pour over the Scriptures with her son Tim when his heart was still tender, still pliable. Too soon, he grew up and left home. And much of Carol's counsel and influence exited with him. Lord, she prayed, give me another chance—another open door with Tim—before he makes a decision that will affect the rest of his and his sweet family's life.

Every Mother's Prayer

Lord,
I want to thank you for helping me see better today. Briefly, I felt that old fearful mindset that sometimes haunts me taking over as I considered the future, my child's future as a married adult. The pain and hurt came rushing back, taking my breath away—literally. Then, as You have done so many other times before, You quieted me from within. And, I rested in You. Remembering your provision, your gentle coaxing love, your tender care for me, Lord, I know your love for me is unequaled.

Still, though I rest in You, I need your courage and wisdom as I walk down memory lane. I want to do this for my child. I need to do this without giving way to fear, or to anger. What's done is done. Today is what matters. And yet I feel You nudging me to bring the former things to mind so that I might teach my own children how to choose more wisely. I am willing to remember. Lord, help me to recall past events in a way that honors You, remembering that You alone are sovereign over all the circumstances in my life. Help me to look back and see your strong hand of protection and provision in the midst of my distress. Even in that, I can bear witness to your mercy and grace, passing it along to my children.

In this world of uncertainty, You alone are our anchor that holds steady. No plan, no purpose, no grand scheme will ever supplant You and your purposes. Thank you, Lord, for bringing renewed hope and birthing a future laced with promise for me and mine. Amen.

Thought for the Day

"We live in a culture that glorifies selfishness more than responsibility. Books and movies urge us to 'follow our hearts,' regardless of our commitments. We need to recapture the beauty of responsibility and the glory of faithfulness. . . . We rarely give ourselves the opportunity to experience the more steadfast satisfaction of loyalty, commitment, and responsibility."

—*Sacred Influence*, by Gary Thomas

Chapter Five

Welcoming Your Extending Family

Guidance for Relating to In-Laws

Be completely humble and gentle; be patient, bearing with one another in love. Make every effort to keep the unity of the Spirit through the bond of peace.
Ephesians 4:2, 3

What constitutes a great day for you? Exactly what essential ingredients make up a day you'll never forget? Does your great day include time with those special people in your family? Is it a place you love? Or maybe it's participating in a favorite activity? Perhaps your idea of a wonderful sunrise to sunset is a problem-free, stress-free, responsibility-free twelve hours or so. But, just how often does that ever happen? In the real world, even on those occasions when every detail is geared for our personal enjoyment and emotional respite, can any of us say it's a perfect day, a perfect relational encounter? Probably not. Even the most meticulously planned event or relational meeting is never completely free of problems, stress, and responsibility.

So what to do? Maybe we need to change our outlook, see the good in the midst of setbacks. And be grateful. See the bigger picture—that there's a world in motion all around us—and tune our eyes into the consequences of being part of it. Perhaps we would all be better off viewing the momentary hiccups in our day as simply that. Temporary. Non-permanent. No-stick. Teflon-type, no-damage-done glitches in an otherwise lovely day. And be grateful.

As we alter our outlook, we also need to look others straight in the eye. What exactly are their needs, wants, and desires? How will my attitudes and actions impact their day? Am I contributing to someone's internal sense of having a "good" day, or am I subtracting from it? Are they grateful for our presence or grateful for our departure? Once we "get it" that life isn't all about us, we can more easily whittle down our choices. Our whole perspective on our days and hours dramatically shifts and lifts. Where we once *expected* and *demanded,* we now generously *offer* and *give*—gratefully.

In the real world, even on those occasions when every detail is geared for our personal enjoyment and emotional respite, can any of us say it's a perfect day, a perfect relational encounter?

No, perfection doesn't exist this side of heaven, but perfect, exquisite moments that clarify vision do. We just have to redefine our terms and open our eyes and heart with gratitude. Instead of trying to frame our world to please ourselves, the truest form of satisfaction is found in giving away, or giving back, what we hold most dear. As we learn to make this important *exchange,* this giving in every way possible, paradoxically, we gain or receive what is more valuable. No, it doesn't make logical sense. But it's true nonetheless.

When Marta opened her front door that early fall morning, she never anticipated being greeted by her mother-in-law standing arms crossed and with a glaring look directed straight at Marta's stunned expression. *What have I done now?* Marta wondered. Without a word, her mother-in-law stormed past her and stood her ground smack dab in the middle of Marta's living room. "Well," she huffed, "I see nothing has changed. This room, this house, is still in the same sorry state it was two days ago. Still filthy, still cluttered, and it's driving my son crazy. What kind of wife and mother are you? You're home all day, can't you manage to keep your own home presentable? And what about meals? Do you even care that Matt works hard all day and comes home not only to this mess but nothing for dinner?"

As the tirade continued, Marta, still too shocked to speak, did one better. She got up and walked into the kitchen and with slow deliberation reached for the metal ring with her extra house, car, and garage keys on it. Slowly, Marta removed her spare front door key and re-entered the living room and handed the key to her mother-in-law. "Here," she said. "If you don't feel I am doing an acceptable job maintaining my home for Matt and the kids, you are more than welcome to clean my house whenever you feel like it." With that, Marta walked herself back into her kitchen and promptly poured herself a cup of coffee—straight, black, and scalding hot. It seemed to fit what she was feeling at that moment.

As she sat sipping her drink, Marta heard the front door close. She wondered all afternoon about that brutal attack: Had her mother-in-law really meant everything she said? Or was she perhaps troubled about something entirely different and attacking Marta was only the release valve for other more serious concerns? Marta didn't know. A big part of her didn't care either.

Interestingly, for the next three weeks her mother-in-law actually came over when Marta was out and cleaned her house from top to bottom. Shocked, Marta didn't really know what to feel at that unexpected response. Still, she decided to keep mum and not engage her mother-in-law further. Marta told herself to consider the free cleaning as a gift, and she did. After the three weeks, Marta came home to a spotless house plus her spare house key placed in the middle of the kitchen table. Never again did her mother-in-law utter a word of complaint (or compliment) about Marta's housekeeping skills. That suited Marta just fine.

So what brought on this memory from years past, years before her divorce from Matt? Marta knew. It was the sometimes edgy tone her new daughter-in-law gave her from time to time. Marta so wanted to be close to her son's new wife. But every attempt to bridge the gap between them seemed doomed from the start. When Jordan first brought Kelly home, the three of them had loads of fun together. They laughed, ate out, enjoyed card games and movies, and shared so many precious conversations. But it all changed once they were married.

Marta had wracked her brain trying to remember some stray comment or unintended slight she might have spoken or done that could have caused this very obvious and painful breach between her and Kelly. But she couldn't recall even a single time when there was ever a problem. Marta didn't want to put her son in the middle, so she had not spoken to Jordan about the growing tension. She did, however, broach the topic with Kelly one afternoon when they were cleaning up the kitchen after a family dinner. But it had gone nowhere. In fact, the way Kelly had blankly stared at Marta made Marta feel like she was crazy, making things up, or becoming an overly-sensitive, overly-protective mother.

Perfection doesn't exist this side of heaven, but perfect, exquisite moments that clarify vision do.

Marta sighed. Jordan was her only child. If and when he and Kelly had children, Marta knew she could very well be cut out of her grandchildren's lives if Kelly and her didn't bridge this gap between them. With nothing left she felt she could do, no other idea coming to her mind, Marta decided to pray, really pray. Beginning now. Marta had always been a diligent intercessor for people in her immediate circle as well as for those who seemed far outside it. All during those early years after she and Matt divorced, Marta relied on her intimate relationship with the Lord in prayer to see her through every hour and every day. It was then that she developed her own "closet of prayer," where she would daily unburden herself of the cares that weighed her down as a single mom. It was there that she learned how powerful and strong and true God's every promise for protection and provision and guidance is.

No better place to take this worry, is there Lord? And how to begin . . . Marta paused. At that moment, she wasn't really feeling too warm toward her daughter-in-law, and yet that still small voice wouldn't let go of a single two word phrase. "Be grateful." What? Be grateful for a tense, difficult relationship? How can I be grateful and thankful when I've done all I can to be the model mother-in-law? Marta's words barely left her lips before she felt again that same inner nudge to give thanks and be grateful. All right, you win, Lord. Despite my emotions, I'm going to right now, on paper, write down all that I am grateful for as it concerns Kelly and this situation. Just for the record, Lord, this is by faith.

So Marta began. The first one was so difficult it actually hurt. The second a mite easier. By the time Marta got to number ten, she could think of five more reasons to give thanks . . . and so she did. Over and over, Marta repeated this daily prayer discipline. Over and over, day by day, Marta obeyed her Lord and gave thanks. After some days, Marta began to see Kelly a bit differently. No, Kelly had not warmed to her more, but somehow Marta had changed and her initial prayer had so grown and blossomed into weightier requests that the way Kelly acted toward her didn't matter so much. And Marta? Well, she just felt grateful for the change taking place within her own heart.

Ready, Set, Adjust!

☀ *Begin every day by giving thanks for at least ten things for which you are grateful.* Sharon was chronically depressed. Had been for years. For as long as she could remember Sharon battled against that dark pit of depression. As a believer, she knew God wanted more for her than constant emotional pain.

She tried to overcome—tried to pray it out of herself—and sometimes Sharon did feel better. But, just like a dark storm cloud, those overwhelming feelings of hopelessness would rush upon her, front and center once again. Until one day. Sharon read a verse about putting on the mantle of praise for the spirit of heaviness. Hmmm . . . putting on and putting off. I can do that. So Sharon began waking up each morning and before she stepped out of bed she gave thanks for ten different things in her life. Funny, she could never stop at ten, and her dark moods . . . well, they never could survive in the presence of such praise and thanksgiving.

☀ *Keep a written record of each thing you give thanks for and date each one.* One of the best gifts Jen's mom gave her as a child was the habit of journaling on a regular basis. For some reason, putting down in black and white everything for which she was grateful helped Jen immensely—especially through the rough times when she didn't have much money for clothes, then college, and even through her own heartbreaking marriage breakup. Jen had so conditioned herself to put on paper the good in her life that it buoyed her up when trying circumstances might have washed her away. Now that her children are all married, Jen has begun making a gratitude list of all she is thankful for in these new relationships. Even though her family doesn't know it, Jen is blessing them and covering each one with a blanket of prayer and protection.

☀ *Ask God to show you how to make His invisible love visible to others.* When Cora was still married, she learned practical ways to cope with her situation, since it didn't seem to make a whit of difference when she complained or groused or demanded her way. What did make a difference was going straight to the Lord for His wise counsel, and then obeying. Cora realized early on that no matter what she did, she might not be able to save her marriage. But she wanted to please the Lord nevertheless. Cora wanted her own life of faith to be a blameless one.

So now she asked the Lord how to be His hands, His feet, and His mouth to her new son-in-law, who frighteningly appears to be very similar to her ex-husband. While it might not stop her son-in-law from behaving in the same negative ways her ex did, Cora still prays that her wayward son-in-law will one day be restored to Christ, in part due to the unconditional love she shows toward him.

☼ *Focus on meeting the needs of others, not your own comfort.* After Sue gets home from work each day, the very last thing she feels like doing is accepting one of her children's requests to babysit her grandchildren for the evening. Much as she loves her kids and grandkids, Sue is getting older, and she's beat after a ten-hour workday. Still, Sue remembers those days as a single mom when she worked all day herself and parented all night. How she relished even two hours of time alone. Even though, thank the Lord, her kids are still married, Sue realizes she can help ensure the healthiness of her kids' marriages by serving them in this way. So . . . she orders pizza for the grandkids, they watch a video, and they all just relax together. Sue knows that time invested in her grandchildren's lives comes full circle, and it also builds solidarity within their entire extended family.

☼ *Don't allow a rocky relationship to define your life or steal your peace of mind.* Rhonda wanted to cry, to scream, to throw something. So she took off her sandals and flung them in the closet. Steaming and frustrated and incredibly hurt, Rhonda couldn't believe it. Not again. How could her daughter-in-law change her mind at the last minute after all the time and money Rhonda had invested in planning this weekend with her grandkids? This had to be the sixth time it had happened in the last six months. Rhonda had had it. No more, she thought. I spent all last evening making reservations, buying special treats, making food, and then she calls and with no explanation and tells me they won't be coming. No explanation! Not even after I asked nicely. And what does my son do? Nothing. Deep breath, Rhonda. You need to breathe and exhale . . . all of it. Feeling hopeless and dejected, Rhonda called her two best friends and they came straight over to console and comfort (and dine) with Rhonda. By evening's end, Rhonda admitted that it wasn't the end of the world to have an inconsiderate daughter-in-law . . . but it wasn't easy either.

✸ *Learn from your past mistakes, don't drown in them.* After Rebekah remarried, she found herself so content in her new marriage. What she didn't bank on were her three new step-daughters who didn't want her married to their father. Though all three girls were married and on their own, Rebekah felt she was fighting an unbeatable battle, trying to win their affections. So after months of extending dinner invitations, offers to babysit, and sending warm cards on special occasions, Rebekah decided to put the situation into the Lord's hands. Whether or not her new stepdaughters ever accept her is no longer her problem. She has tried to "make peace" and live peaceably with them. And in years past, Rebekah just about killed herself trying to please everyone she knew. Now she lets go. Yes, Rebekah continues to pray, but she no longer carries the burden of trying to make peace with those who are not willing or able to recip-rocate. Rebekah has learned that prayer yields higher dividends and fewer physical stresses.

✸ *Live with a "one day at a time" mentality.* "Today is the only day I am responsible for." This is the mantra Noelle re-peats aloud every morning as she gets ready for work. She is by no means a pushover, yet she had agreed to allow first one son and then the other to move in with her while their re-spective homes were being updated and built. With her two sons and their wives now living at home again, Noelle often feels usurped and pushed aside even in her own home. While her house is large enough to accommodate four extra adults, Noelle often wonders if her psyche can be equally accommodating. She now fully understands the old adage, two cooks in a kitchen is one too many. Noelle wisely decided to refrain from becoming involved in the verbal wrangling between her two daughters-in-law. She gave them space—her space actually. But this was fine; in three months, Noelle would be waving goodbye to her sons and their wives, hopefully with all their relationships still intact.

 Give thanks daily, hourly, minute by minute. After Joy's father died, then her mother nine months later, she found herself struggling to maintain emotional closeness with her daughters and their spouses. All that pain, in such a short period of time, left Joy shell-shocked and emotionally fragile. It didn't help that both of her sons-in-law were boisterous, bold, and outspoken about what they thought was ailing Joy. She cringed when she knew they were expected to arrive. Sometimes her anxiety grew so intense, Joy's heart would beat uproariously, leaving her exhausted and worn out, even before the visit.

What to do? Joy dug into scripture and began reciting verses that spoke of God's will and giving thanks, of His mercy and grace being enough for every moment, every challenge, emotional or otherwise. Once she began this exercise, Joy almost . . . just almost . . . began looking forward to her daughters' announcement that they were intending to visit just so she could have some prep time meditating on God's good promises. It was good medicine for her broken heart.

✹

Every Mother's Prayer

Lord,
Here I am once again reliving part of my former life that I always prayed I would never, ever have to repeat. Seems like no matter how long or far I travel, similar issues revisit themselves in my life.

If there is some hidden attitude or lesson I've yet to learn, please show me now. I still feel keenly the pain of rejection and criticism from my past marriage. Now, to have yet another person treat me with contempt feels like too much to bear. Will you help me, Lord? I truly want to honor You through the entirety of my life, through every relationship, every bump and curve . . . I want You to be front and center. Help me to see myself accurately and not be blindsided by my own sin. If I have offended, then let me seek forgiveness and work toward restoration. Lord, by faith, though it pains me to do so, I am going to give thanks for this situation. I am determined to love without reserve, no matter what. Give me eyes that see. Ears that hear. A heart that beats in time with another's pain, and make me willing to lose my life for You, for others, without reserve. I do thank You now. For I know and am confident that You do promise to bring good out of even the most painful of circumstances . . . in Your time. Teach me how to pray, pray, and pray some more, investing in the lives of my children and their spouses in this most holy way. Amen.

Thought for the Day

"The awesome reward of the interceding life is just this: the pleasure of God poured out upon us as we meet with Him at the mercy seat in prayer for others. Following Jesus, who entered the holy place once for all through His own blood, we, too, lay down our lives and draw near with a sincere heart and full assurance of faith and, in so doing, move the heart of our heavenly Father. (Hebrews 9:12; 10:22)"

—*Intimate Intercession: The Sacred Joy of Praying for Others,* by Tricia McCary Rhodes

Chapter Six

Assessing Career and Educational Options

Insights for a Promising Tomorrow

> *For the Spirit God gave us does
> not make us timid, but gives us
> power, love and self-discipline.*
> 2 Timothy 1:7

On any given day, single moms across the nation will be caught daydreaming about tomorrow. Not that daydreaming is a bad exercise; sometimes the most winning plans have been hatched during these mental wanderings. The kind of musing that hinders rather than helps a single mother reach her goals is different. This troublesome visitor incites disappointment, frustration, and impatience. It never allows for the beauty of one's present life to hold sway. Author David Ireland writes in his book *Secrets of a Satisfying Life,* "One of the greatest life lessons you can ever learn is to enjoy life through the process of attaining your goals" (103).

While there might not be any hard evidence to support this fact, it's pretty clear that society in general places a weighty amount of pressure on women—all women, moms or not—to succeed on many levels, both personal and professional. Today's single mom will necessarily hold multiple roles, each one vying for her attention and interest. If she's smart, she recognizes the fact that today's responsibilities do not define her life as a whole. Life can change in an instant, and often does. There is something to be said for getting into the rhythm of your days. It is important to view life, the few-and-far-between glamorous moments as well as the more mundane yet serviceable bulk of daily responsibilities, as all worthwhile.

Society in general places a weighty amount of pressure on women . . . to succeed on many levels, both personal and professional.

Everything we do in the next twenty-four hours prepares us in some way for tomorrow. Whether we long for greatness in some obscure professional field or simply hanker to excel at gardening matters little. Our focus, our intent, must be on giving our all today in pursuit of whatever we turn our attention toward.

Sadly, countless mothers spend precious time wandering mentally into tomorrow's unknown, feeding feelings of discontent that eventually override their good sense. Yes, today's difficulties do take a toll. Still, armed with the right outlook, women can use today's hardships as stepping-stones to future success. It's all in one's viewpoint and ultimate goal. Learning to take everything in its turn enables women to invest in today's work while eyeing hopeful possibilities for tomorrow. Author David Ireland reminds women that as we seek to live fully on this given day, "the destination seems nearer and the view is more picturesque" (103). It is possible to be totally present in the now and still have a vision for tomorrow. It is!

Kathryn was getting off early. Smile. How long had it been since she actually walked in the door of her house before 8:00 p.m.? Long time. So tonight Kathryn decided to celebrate. A little. She stopped by the deli and picked up a broasted chicken, her favorite locally made hummus, and even treated herself to a small tub of coffee ice cream. Wonderful. That and some very faint background jazz would set her to rights in no time. Not that Kathryn really had anything to grumble about. Not today, especially not today. It's just that . . . what? she mused. It had been a terribly long, drawn-out journey to what happened today. To being promoted to her bank's managerial position. Had it been worth it? Absolutely. And yet, she had doubts. More times than she could recall, Kathryn had doubted and wondered and weighed every alternative. Uncertain, unsure, unable to see what the future might hold, Kathryn had done the best she could given the resources available to her. Thinking back, Kathryn took a small pleasure in enumerating the multi-faceted obstacles she had overcome. Limited expendable income. Little "extra" time for pursuing a college degree while raising her son. Virtually no energy reserves to call upon when life threw curveballs from every direction.

Kathryn smiled. Again. Remembering. Bringing to mind what assets she had. Still has. Friends. A few loyal friends who stuck by her, cheered her on, and prayed with her (for her) with a fearsome tenacity that frequently left Kathryn speechless. Expectant. Excited. Ready to hit the books again, write that next paper, and prepare a speech. All those little "things" added up over time so that Kathryn ended up with a bachelors degree in business just about the same time her son graduated from the college he attended. Funny how life works out.

More ironic still is how the very worst that happens to us has the potential to eventually morph into something really quite amazing and beautiful. Kathryn wondered at her life, all the dips and turns along the way, they might have short-circuited me, but they didn't. Why? From all earthly reasoning, I should have failed. Big time. My beginning surely wasn't so impressive. Married, divorced, remarried, had a son. Then abandoned. How Kathryn despised that single word. But hate it though she might, it aptly described her situation. No other word felt so true to what Kathryn had endured when her second husband simply disappeared, leaving her with little money, a barely-there education, and no warning. None. Kathryn didn't know if she'd live through the shock of it all. And with Bobbie only four years old, Kathryn was paralyzed by worry, fear, and escalating panic attacks.

If it hadn't been for her next-door neighbor, Gina, who daily, sometimes hourly, coaxed Kathryn's anxieties away with a potent elixir of prayer, unconditional love, and her can't-say-no-to-chocolate-chip cookies, Kathryn was certain she would have given in to despair. Gina, God's angel in the guise of a widowed, plainspoken but kindly hearted, Christ-follower. The first one to speak real truth, hard truth to Kathryn. There wasn't a day that Kathryn didn't pray a silent word of thanks for her dear friend. And who was the one to first put the notion of Kathryn finishing college into her head? Who was it who helped her "ready up" for her first interview at the bank? Who babysat for Bobbie when he was sick or when school was out? Gina. It was as though God plopped Gina right square in front of Kathryn expressly to meet this new single mom's desperate and often relentless never-ending laundry list of needs.

Once Kathryn landed her full-time teller position, once she got acclimated to working again, there was Gina, nudging her to start eyeing the lead teller job . . . in time. At first, Kathryn pooh-poohed Gina's suggestions, dismissing them as pipe dreams. But over time, as her confidence swelled, Kathryn gave more thought to Gina's counsel. Get busy finishing your degree, one class at a time if need be, and prove your worth at the bank. Make them notice you, Gina encouraged. So Kathryn did. Months into years, and gradually Kathryn's work ethic and her skill did get noticed and rewarded. From lead teller to assistant manager and there Kathryn stayed for the last five years. Until her boss moved out of state, and Kathryn moved up. Bank manager. Gina was right. One small step, one day at a time, one way or another, you'll make it. Thanks, Gina.

The very worst that happens to us has the potential to eventually morph into something really quite amazing and beautiful.

Stop your daydreaming girl, you need to make some calls! First, get Bobbie on the phone with the good news right now. He'll be so pleased. And Gina, I'll call her from home later tonight. Wait a minute. I can just hear Gina scolding me. News like this cannot be delivered over the telephone line. It's got to be in person or nothing! Okay, so it's one more stop to make before home. It wouldn't be a celebration without Gina, now would it? This is as much her promotion as it is mine.

Ready, Set, Adjust!

☼ *Exhausted or energized: in every area of life be careful to balance work and rest—mental, emotional, and physical.* Elizabeth downed her fourth, count 'em, fourth cup of coffee and it was only 11:00 in the morning. That, and her daily long-standing staple of a white bagel for breakfast, was what she relied on to keep her going through the busy rush at the coffee shop where she worked as a barista. Elizabeth saw all types come in for their own early morning caffeine jolt and recognized the symptoms—none very positive. Sipping the last dregs of her favorite bean, Elizabeth decided to reform a few of her not-so-healthy habits. Instead of drinking enough liquid energy to see her through her day, she tried hitting the treadmill in the mornings and eating a breakfast with protein and complex carbs. If I ever want to run my own shop, she mused, I need to take care of me—body and soul—first.

☼ *Purposeless or purposeful: dream big and then make your plans practical.* These days Megan had a difficult time making a decision about what to prepare for dinner, let alone trying to decide what major to choose at her local community college. Grimacing in painful recollection, Megan had been so embarrassed when the counselor started quizzing her on her career goals. Goals? Career? What goals? What career? Megan wanted to laugh or cry. In all honesty, Megan simply wanted to stay home with her kids and be a full-time mom but that wasn't possible anymore. Push had come to shove and Megan needed to get food on the table and pay the mortgage . . . or at least supplement what her ex-husband was sending her way. Sitting in that counselor's office jolted Megan into the realization that on her own she couldn't decide, there had been far too many decisions this past year. So, in not deciding, Megan made a choice. She realized she needed to gather her family and friends together and ask for their input, their help, and their expertise. Everyone keeps offering to help me, and I've never known what to say. But this . . . this feels so big, so overwhelming. I do need direction, and a plan that will work.

☼ *Unreasonable expectations or sensible intent: be satisfied with doing the best you can.* Teri had a problem. As the retail manager of an upscale clothier in her town's "better" shopping mall, Teri had to be exact. She recognized that in order to succeed, she had to maintain high standards for herself, her employees, and her kids, grown though they were. Yet these standards all too often spilled over into what Teri too generously termed her "mothering." No doubt, even a brief glance at Teri's obvious success gave others pause to consider her words of advice. While she could finesse her customers to no end, plying them with compliments and persuasive enticements, the tactic didn't work with those who were close to her. Teri, at heart, simply wanted her family to succeed. It terrified Teri even to consider that her now adult offspring might have to "go without" as she did in those years after the divorce. Teri had spent the last ten years making sure no one she loved would ever be in the same financial straits she had suffered through. But what Teri failed to grasp was that, even though her initial intent to work toward financial independence was a good desire, it had morphed into obsession. Life cannot be encapsulated into single-digit dimensions. Teri has yet to realize that a "good life" as defined by a biblical worldview is always multi-faceted. And that suffering, even in the financial realm, isn't necessarily as catastrophic to the soul as Teri's self-imposed anxiety-laden existence.

☼ *Shortsighted or perceptive visionary: refuse to see today's shortfall as the last or final word.* Andrea, a widowed former owner of a quaint bed and breakfast was ready to re-open her previously defunct business. After having spent the last three years taking care of her elderly mother, Andrea was now free to "do business" on her own terms again. Though Andrea's former foray into the business world had ended with little financial gain, Andrea had learned so much in the interim. Spending those long hours giving care in her mother's home gave Andrea ample time to read and study and prepare. And to recognize where she'd made mistakes the first time around. Now she was ready and her bank was willing to extend enough cash to do some needed renovations before she opened her beloved family homestead to the public again. Looking back, that end of the dream experience wasn't the end at all, it was only a stage in the journey. But, I'm not staying in that place, Andrea determined, I'm moving forward.

☼ *Selfish or other-minded: discipline yourself to look beyond your own wants/needs/desires.* Allison raised her son and daughter to think of others first. Sadly, she wasn't mirroring her own words. Though she worked herself through college while parenting her kids, Allison also treated herself to what she called "escapes," comprised of extravagant evenings out, weekend getaways with fellow nurses, and shopping, shopping, shopping. In a word, Allison was self-minded. What started out as being gone in the evenings for class requirements led to a pattern where Allison was never home, never even seemed to care where her college-age son and daughter were, or what they were doing. From Allison's viewpoint, she'd paid her dues, now it was her time. Thankfully, her kids cared enough to confront their mom, telling her they might be adults by legal definition, but they still wanted (and needed) a mom who was there for them.

✹ *Haphazard or methodical: focus does matter.* Maria is a dabbler. One month she's into this project, the next month she's immersed in something else. It wouldn't be so bad if Maria could confine her fickleness to hobbies alone. No, Maria whimsically decides to change career paths just as often. Her friends never know what to expect from her. So, after almost having to declare bankruptcy for the third time, Maria's friends decided an "intervention" was in order. Together, they were going to kidnap Maria for an entire day and hold her hostage at her home. While they had a captive audience, her friends would feed her, encourage her, and then talk tough with her. Then they'd brainstorm together some practical ways to get Maria on track and keep her there. Each of Maria's pals knew full well that only with consistent accountability and lots of verbal "way to go's" would Maria at last find the freedom that comes from an ordered life.

✹ *Stubbornly independent or humbly teachable: learn to listen well to those who know.* Linda works hard as a police dispatcher; she is a strong, well organized, never-gets-ruffled type of gal. Emergencies don't send Linda over the edge: they get her blood going. She loves her job. Thrives on it. But Linda hasn't always been in such a pleasant work situation. For years she worked as an at-home phone representative selling add-ons to the cable company's current customers. Linda complained to anyone who would listen about how she despised her job. She couldn't get enthused about bundling various products together, nor could she get excited about this month's special offer. Linda wanted to make a difference. But the only difference she made was making others miserable with her grousing. Finally, her best friend Edie said "Enough! Get out there and find a job that uses your skills to their best advantage . . . and do it today. Please!" So Linda took a career assessment test online and was happily surprised to find on the list of suitable jobs for her temperament and personality the previously unconsidered career of emergency dispatcher. Everyone who knows and loves Linda is so happy that Edie stepped up and spoke up—more important, that Linda listened.

※ *Unrealistic self image or knowledgeable self awareness: know yourself inside and out.* Natalie cleaned office buildings for a living, thank you very much. Always had. Throughout her single parenting years, Natalie believed she had the best of both worlds. And she did. For Natalie, cleaning offices at night meant she could be home before her children left for school (now college) or their jobs, then she slept during the day, and was up again by early evening to enjoy dinner and attend their sporting events before she left for work at 11:00 p.m. Did it work for everyone? Not a chance. But Natalie appreciated the stillness of working when others were not around. She often had her earplugs in, listening to this or that tape, and when she'd had enough listening to instructional or inspirational material, she would put her iPod away and listen to God. Natalie, laboring in those quiet hours Monday through Friday, didn't see it as a hardship to work through the night. She understood herself better than most. She liked the alone time! And, Natalie saw God's hand of provision throughout the situation.

Every Mother's Prayer

Lord,
How do I begin to voice what I feel so deep within? Saying thank you simply isn't enough. Speaking, or attempting to put into words, what I know to be true seems to cheapen the love you have bestowed on me. I am overwhelmed by your mercy, your grace. I am . . . undone. Unworthy. So humbled. All those long seasons of working and wrestling

and hanging on by my fingernails . . . you were there. Cheering me on. Telling my heart to stay with the task you had appointed me to. You spoke for me when I could not speak for myself. And then raised up other voices to speak for me, to me, words of truth, of hope, and of conviction. Amazing. I never had to doubt long, before one of your faithful children would sidle up beside me and offer me exactly what I needed to hear. All this love . . . for me.

Oh Lord, as I stand here in gratitude and gratefulness . . . on the other side of those early struggles . . . let me never forget the battle itself. In my heart, I believe it is imperative that I remember, and remember well, how you interceded on my behalf. I have come a long way, this earthly life is not easy. And though I am experiencing welcome relief from my toil today, I am not so naïve as to think tomorrow will be as kind. Tomorrow will be a fresh opportunity, possibly a new direction, for me to choose wisely. Please be close by at every juncture, making your will and your way plain to me. In every way, every day, help me to be sober, alert, watchful, and ready, relying on you for my very breath of life. You alone are the enabler. Your mercies truly never cease; they are new each morning. For that alone I praise your name. Amen.

Thought for the Day

"How big is your God? Big enough to intervene? Big enough to be trusted? Big enough to be held in awe and ultimate respect? Big enough to erase your worries and replace them with peace? When your God is too small, your problems are magnified and you retreat in fear and insecurity. When your God is great, your problems pale into insignificance and you stand in awe as you worship the King. Which are you—a little Godder? Or a big Godder?"

—*Job: A Man of Heroic Endurance*, by Charles Swindoll

Chapter Seven

Instilling Financial Stability
Preparations for Today and Tomorrow

So do not worry, saying, "What shall we eat?" or
"What shall we drink?" or "What shall we wear?"
For the pagans run after all these things, and
your heavenly Father knows that you need them.
But seek first his kingdom and his righteousness,
and all these things will be given to you as well.
Matthew 6:31–33

*E*ver observed a person's behavior once she admitted out loud she needed to change something in her life? It's a fascinating process. An individual begins by first removing those cumbersome mental objections. She now realizes the harm of her "habit," which could play out in real life as either engaging in a specific practice or failing to do so. In either case, a woman starts to mentally recast her life: she pictures her life with or without this particular focal point as a better one.

Remember though, change that endures begins above the neck. Think about it. How often has a friend or colleague started a diet, gone back to school, moved cross country, ended a relationship, without adequate mental prep and have it succeed during those early "detox" days and weeks? Doesn't happen very often. It's crucial to think, think, and think some more, before, during, and after making key changes. And moms are great for thinking . . . and often over-thinking.

Those women who make lasting (and positive) changes in their lives do so after spending some generous chunks of time ruminating about the consequences before they act. They look ahead and count the cost from every vantage point. They anticipate possible pitfalls and stumbling blocks, as

It's crucial to think, think, and think some more, before, during, and after making key changes. And moms are great for thinking . . . and often over-thinking.

well as temptations to give up (or give in to). One by one, individuals "erase" any mental objections to delving into a new course of action. For indeed there are actual costs to be reckoned with as well as potential ones. When a woman decides to exercise, it will necessitate a sacrifice of time and energy and demand a payout of self-discipline and persistence. Getting out of the credit card debt debacle requires saying no to impulsive spending while countering spur of the moment indulgences with thoughtful financial planning. Repairing a fractured relationship will dictate an investment of time and emotion while looking for solutions to strengthen and shore up the shaky association.

See the connection here? It's all about considering and counting the cost. Then deliberately deciding to take the leap. It's risky to embrace change and sometimes it just plain hurts. But the long-term payoffs, even amidst setbacks, are all worthwhile, strength-building exercises set in motion today for a financially healthier tomorrow. Single moms, in particular, are already pretty savvy in the counting-the-cost department. So for them, learning to grow financially savvy (and secure) over the long haul means embracing an all encompassing pause, plan, and then proceed formula.

Emma wasn't prepared for this evening's meeting. She knew she was going to get scolded by her accountant. Well, for goodness sake, at least she now had an accountant! That's an improvement, right?

For years, Emma's financial portfolio resembled a hobbyist's first attempt at scrapbooking. Bits and pieces tossed in here and there, colorful, yes, but not very polished and presentable. But Emma had learned her lesson. She had. Indeed.

After Emma became a single mom, she and daughter Courtney had a grand old time. In between the awful times, that is. I mean the isn't-it-almost-payday, we're-running-low-on-food-in-the-house-and-the-electricity-could-go-off-at-any-second kind of awful. Emma realized she should do better. She was the sole responsible adult in the house now. But it was hard to say no, to herself and to Courtney. They had both suffered . . . it was true, they had suffered.

So when Emma sold a new house or a pricey piece of real estate and that "extra" money came rolling in, she struggled not to spend part of it. Okay, all of it. Seemed like Courtney as a thirteen-year-old growing teen was constantly in need of something new in the clothing department. And then there were shoes, accessories, makeup, and even a flourishing interest in hair color, cuts, and waves. Weren't these all things her daughter needed? Emma thought so. And her bank statement was proof of what Emma deemed most important.

Emma and her bank had a . . . well . . . delicate, occasionally even problematical, relationship because of the way they clumsily danced around each other at the end of every calendar month. Emma would be late on her mortgage, habitually so. The bank manager would then place a reminder call to Emma personally since she knew Emma outside their business relationship. On a good day, this merciful manager could catch Emma at home on the first or second try. On a not-so-good day, she would spend days trying to reach Emma at either her home or on her cell. Depending upon

It's risky to embrace change and sometimes it just plain hurts. But the long-term payoffs, even amidst setbacks, are all worthwhile, strength-building exercises set in motion today for a financially healthier tomorrow.

whether or not Emma anticipated a sizable incoming paycheck, she would answer the call . . . or not.

To Emma's credit (as a morally responsible human being), she always felt tremendous guilt for not immediately returning the bank's summons. But after that instantaneous reaction of guilt, Emma would one minute feel surges of anger toward her ex, whom she blamed for getting her into "this fix" in the first place, and the next minute be pointing the finger back at herself for being foolish enough to spend beyond her means whenever the mood struck her. And her moods struck—fast and furiously.

From Emma's perspective there was no way out. She truly didn't have the financial training from childhood into adulthood to handle the daily discipline of setting up and maintaining a budget. It frustrated her to no end. And when Emma grew frustrated, she spent. Added to her inability to organize an ongoing reliable bill-paying system was her growing anxiety over the future. Retirement specifically. What will it be like when I'm living on a fixed income? she worried. I can't work forever. Not that I would even want to. If I don't do something now, make some significant changes that will set me and my meager savings account in a different direction, I'm pretty well doomed. At least Emma was now being honest, facing the hard facts of her position. But what to do?

Emma's first and best step was to return that call from her banker friend. And apologize. Sincerely. Repeatedly. Next, she set up a meeting with her banker and together they held a financial snapshot meeting reviewing Emma's assets and liabilities (her spending habits being one of them). Once they clearly understood how Emma's bills compared with her monthly income, her banker suggested a few financial advisors/accountants who would help Emma get out of debt and stay there. It helped that her banker warned Emma of possible—and likely—eventual foreclosure on her home. Emma gasped. Then and there this single mom saw the seriousness of the situation for what it was. No way, no how, can I lose this home . . . at least not because I'm so undisciplined that I can't put a stop to frivolous spending.

So nine months after Emma's epiphany moment, she sat dutifully awaiting the arrival of her accountant. She sort of liked that notion, "her accountant," because it sort of reassured her that she was becoming financially responsible. Like most other adults she knew. It felt good even though all her financial documents weren't in perfect pristine order and yes, she might get scolded a bit. Still, Emma was positively sure she was on the right track now. No outstanding credit card statements. No overdue bills. And a small but "in the black" checking account that was inching upwards by the month. Emma was hoping for (and working toward) the goal of being in a position to actually invest a portion of her income at the year-end mark. *Tonight just might be the turning point I've been waiting for,* she thought hopefully. *Now, let's see if I can at least make a good attempt at getting these papers in proper order before that meeting.*

Ready, Set, Adjust!

Step back, literally and figuratively, and evaluate your life. Don't be afraid to retrace your steps (or make an about-face) in an effort to step into positive plans for the future. Angie wasn't sure about moving back in with her mom after all these years of living on her own. But she realized that it wasn't cost-efficient to continue living in her four-bedroom home by herself. She had briefly considered asking another single mom to move in and share expenses, but again, Angie wasn't sure she would feel comfortable living with a friend, even a good friend. On the other hand, Angie and her mom got along well together. Neither one was intrusive or overbearing. It might work. Her mom's home was certainly big enough to accommodate most of Angie's favorite home furnishings too. Angie's mom had "made room" for this very possibility when she revamped the house a few years back, when Angie's dad required wheelchair access to the house. They even had a contractor build an in-laws attached bungalow . . . for themselves. Always thinking ahead, that's my mom, Angie smiled. Now, Dad's gone and Mom prefers the smaller cordoned-off section of the house to ensure her own privacy. She knows my kids will be visiting on weekends, and she, like me, wants a private place of retreat. Since Mom doesn't want to leave the family homestead and I want to leave an inheritance to my kids, this just might be the best way to achieve both ends.

✺ *Research and record a new plan of action. Invite others who are succeeding at what you want to do to act as your guides, mentors, and cheerleaders (or you can learn by their mistakes).* Helen felt stuck. Even though she had recently been offered a promotion at work in the HR department at her city's most reputable senior facilitator, Helen wanted more flexibility to travel and to visit her out-of-town grandchildren. Though she had worked hard to get to the place where she could run the department, Helen now wondered if that's what she truly wanted. She'd watched a friend and colleague's life alter dramatically after taking a similar post, and Helen remembered promising herself never to give in to the temptation of a more prestigious position at the cost of sacrificing her private life. This promotion, if Helen accepted it, would demand longer hours through the week and some on-call weekends. She took a good long, hard look at her finances; even though this promotion meant a raise, it would detract from her quality of life. No, Helen determined, I have enough to live and retire on. Five years ago, before my kids had kids, I might have jumped at this promotion. But today, it just doesn't seem to matter that much to me. My goals have changed, so have my priorities. Any gain in money would be a loss in precious freedom and flexibility, and you can't quantify time spent with people you love.

❋ **Move toward change and ask for accountability.** One decision (or action) at a time (no matter how small) is a positive shift. At forty-nine, Tonya's feet hurt. She had been a waitress for as many years as she could remember. And yes, though she worked at an upscale fine-dining establishment where the tips were excellent, Tonya hadn't taken into account (until she broke her ankle and was off work for three months) that she lacked a retirement fund. Tonya realized, as she spent time off recovering, that even though she had saved through the years and paid for everything in cash, she wouldn't have much financial cushion once she retired. It was time, way past time, to listen to her dad's advice and get with his financial advisor. Her dad was always telling Tonya there were some simple steps she could take now, in the form of small monthly investments, that would yield a sizable cash reserve later. Trouble was, Tonya should have listened to this counsel years earlier, but she'd always had another use for the money. Okay, Tonya resolved, today I am going to make an appointment and see about getting automatic monthly deductions. Maybe that way it will be easier to stick with the plan long term. If I don't see and feel the cash in hand, then I won't be tempted to use it other places.

❋ **Make out a will and plan funeral expenses.** Marisa didn't like to think about her own death. But . . . after her parents died within nine months of one another, she realized how essential (and thoughtful to the remaining family members) it was to have a will in place and a funeral already planned and paid for in advance. Marisa's heart was so broken when her folks died in such a short period of time, the very last thing she wanted was to sit in a lawyer's office trying to piece together their estate and assets. And then sit in a funeral home (twice), trying to decide among the many options available, how to best implement her parents' taste, preferences, and beliefs at the memorial. It just about broke her heart—and her wallet—

when the funeral expenses came due before their estate was settled through probate. And to think—all of this trouble might have been avoided had they planned ahead. Marisa gave herself some time to heal and grieve, but she also made plans to take care of this business so that her children wouldn't have to endure what she had.

✸ *Reestablish a line of credit.* Lori had never even considered that after having been married for over six years she didn't have her own line of credit. None. Everything had been in her ex-husband's name. Sure, his credit was excellent, but Lori had none. She never thought about it until she went to make her first large purchase after their divorce and was turned down by the credit card agency when she applied. Lori was stunned. Couldn't anyone get a credit card these days? Yes and no. While Lori had never missed paying a bill through her checking account—her joint checking account that is—as a stay-at-home mom, she didn't have her own credit rating. Nothing. So, Lori began to establish her own credit history by starting out small. Another lesson learned: don't assume anything when it comes to finances, she thought wryly.

✸ *Review how marital assets are filed.* When Lindsay's husband divorced her after twenty-plus years of marriage, she received one-half of his estate and one-half of his retirement fund. To Lindsay's shock, a few weeks after her husband passed away, she received a call from a government office saying she was entitled to over nine hundred dollars a month from a fund he had paid into during their marriage. Lindsay was shocked, but elated. Then she got to thinking about how little she really understood about her financial rights after the divorce. If she had been in real need and had not been contacted by this agency, what a loss that would have been! An unnecessary loss . . . all because she was ignorant of the marital assets she is legally entitled to.

✹ *Develop realistic expectations in caring for elderly relatives.*
Karen was one of six adult children, none of whom lived in the same hometown as Karen and their elderly parents. Up until recently, her eighty-year-old mom and dad were fit, mobile, and able to care for themselves. But of late, only her dad drove the car, and he couldn't see well enough to drive after dark . . . or in inclement weather . . . or right after he put his drops in his eyes, which he frequently did right before calling Karen to please take them to an appointment they had neglected to tell her about. Little things, really. But they were adding up to significant chunks of time for Karen. Time spent away from her kids and from managing her own work and responsibilities at home. Karen knew she couldn't afford to hire help for her folks on her salary alone. She began thinking about how much of the responsibility for their care was falling on her shoulders. How much should? Karen fretted and fumed for awhile, complaining that her brothers and sisters did precious little to help their parents out. If they can't be here, they can at the least send in reinforcements by helping me plan and hire out some of these tasks. Tonight, I'm going to email them and call a family meeting ASAP. Together—and Karen meant it—together we'll delegate specific areas of responsibility to each one of us.

✹ *Allocate funds for your children's college and wedding expenses.* Ashley had three daughters and a son. Adding up in her head all the future expenses of four grown kids was a terrifying venture. How on earth would she ever find the money to send them all to college—not to mention potential wedding expenses. Shoulders slumped. Ashley realized she was in way over her head to figure this one out. So she called in the troops, as she affectionately referred to her three closest single-mom friends. As the youngest in the group, Ashley frequently brainstormed with these women everything from fixing a flat tire to finding the best health insurance provider in town. Between them, I'm sure they have some tried and true resources for me to investigate now while the kids are still in high school. Ashley breathed a little easier just knowing there were others who had tackled these seemingly impossible money hurdles before her. There was help out there. Ashley just needed to make the right connections.

Every Mother's Prayer

Lord,

I'm not sure where to begin. I feel as though I've wandered around for so long, trying to get a real handle on this whole issue of money and finances and planning for the future and trusting in your care. Where does one begin and the other end? I do believe that your Word assures me that all my needs will be met. I believe this. And yet, I also realize that I am responsible for making certain I am a wise steward of all you've given me to manage. Which means, I must make prudent plans. I must take into account my tomorrows based upon my income today. Lord, help me. Bring skilled and able helpers my way to guide my steps and to teach me how to best prepare and invest. I want to sleep well at night, confident that I've fulfilled my responsibility both in taking action and by resting in your promised provision. Again, I ask for your help, your grace, that extra measure of faith I am so in need of. Lord, please draw near to me and fill my heart and mind with good reminders of your past care for me. Make me a woman of faith who has vision to provide not just for my needs but to give generously to those around me. Thank you, Lord, for your good word of hope, your Holy Spirit of comfort, and your abiding presence at my side. At all times—rich, poor, and everything in between—I know You are standing with me, for me. Amen.

Thought for the Day

"Money isn't the issue. In and of itself, money is just a form of exchange. Our trust in almighty God is the issue. Most people believe money is the link to their security, power, self-worth, and happiness. In essence, money is the means to that end. However, this is distinctly opposed to what God wants for us. God wants us to rely on Him for our security, power, self-worth, and joy."

—*God Is My Success: Transforming Adversity Into Your Destiny,* by Larry Julian

Chapter Eight

Welcoming the Next Generation
The Precious Gift of Grandparenting

> *You did not choose me, but I chose you and*
> *appointed you so that you might go and bear*
> *fruit—fruit that will last—and so that whatever*
> *you ask in my name the Father will give*
> *you. This is my command: Love each other.*
> John 15:16–17

All grown up now? With better things to do? Weightier matters pressing upon you, shadowing you? Merciless time crunches, dire financial gymnastics, strained work relationships? Feeling pressured on every side to comply or conform? Oh, wake up and stop murmuring about the everyday stresses and woes we all have. There are more important things to be done.

Stop everything. Quiet that frenzied hamster wheel in your mind. Forget about deadlines, details, debts, and any other impending disaster that tempts you away from the most significant thing on today's agenda. For the next few moments just sit back and consider: What is the most valuable quantifiable asset you possess? If you're toying with mental pictures of a mini-mansion, that sports car sitting in your garage, a summer trip to Europe, or even the newest technological wonder, halt. These accruements don't even come close to measuring up to the *most important whatever* in a person's life, at least by any honest mother's standards.

Try again. Here's a hint. Your most priceless resource can't be begged, borrowed, or stolen from you. It's so indefinably precious that all seek it, long for its company, and yet for some it remains elusive. Doesn't matter if you're rich or poor; it's an equal opportunity blessing. It all begins and ends with you. Give up? It is relationship. It is family. Children. Grandchildren. What matters most is our connection to others. Our eternal investment into the lives of those under our loving care.

Won't make much difference ten years from now whether you moved into the nicer neighborhood you're eyeing, joined that elite country club, or finally achieved a coveted position of status in your workplace. If you don't have the good sense to keep up with family, nurturing these vital relationships over the long haul, you'll be alone. No one there to share the joy of accomplishment. Many things in life will change. Life is at best uncertain. Tomorrow's circumstances may very well alter your plans for the future. So who will be there to stand beside you when life sounds the death knell? Who will you run to when the pain reaches beyond your ability to cope? You'll turn to your children, your grandchildren, for solace and support. And the best part is this: they will be there for you. But are you willing to set aside some of "your" time now that is truly time for them?

Consider family relationships the best "life" insurance policy you'll ever invest in. The dividends, the returns, are well above and beyond the cost. Before the day is out, choose to connect, to invest, and to love. Before the sun goes down, choose wisely, for your sake and that of your family. So send an e-mail (or drop by) to a close-by child or grandchild and make a date to meet within the next week. Send another e-mail (or make a phone call) to faraway loved ones, just to check up on them. Then send one to your own address, re-

Your most priceless resource can't be begged, borrowed, or stolen from you. It's so indefinably precious that all seek it, long for its company, and yet for some it remains elusive.

minding yourself of the sweet joy family has brought your way. And be glad to have been given the opportunity both to choose and be chosen for the task of loving your children, your grandchildren.

Isobel was a grandmother. What wonder she felt. Her son's first child. A baby girl. Kylie. She couldn't believe it. From head to toe, pure bliss. That's what Isobel felt when she first heard the joyous news. She couldn't quite grasp the fact that her son Jeff Jr. was now a father. Isobel brought back to her own memory tender mental pictures from that day so long ago when she first discovered she was pregnant with Jeff. How did twenty-seven years pass so quickly? Like a whisper on the wind. Here and gone before she realized it.

I'm a grandmother, Isobel said aloud just for the fun of it. How wonderfully exciting this is going to be! I'll be able to love little Kylie without all the distractions and responsibilities of parenting her. Now there's a win-win situation if ever there was one. How glad I am that Jeff decided to wait until after graduating from college to get married. And then hold off two more years before starting his family. It was just good, simple, smart planning on their part, Isobel thought gratefully. Unlike me . . . way back when. She glowered, remembering.

What was I thinking? Jeffrey and I sure didn't look to our own future very well. We got married in a rush and plowed headlong into every marital pressure-cooker scenario under the sun. He was still in school. I worked full-time. I got pregnant, unexpectedly, which put us in a financial bind. Jeff wouldn't finish school for another two years after our baby was born. Isobel shuddered as she recalled having to drop baby Jeff off at daycare that first morning. Pure torture . . . for both of them, she loved her little guy so much . . . it broke her heart not to be spending her days and nights with him. And that was only the beginning of Isobel's quick-step dance between work responsibilities, parenting her beloved son, and trying to please Jeffrey.

I should have known that something was going to give way. And it did. Our marriage. Too much, too soon. And neither of us equipped to handle life's obstacles at the time. So I single-handedly parented Jeff from elementary school on. Jeffrey was there too, but it wasn't the same as having two parents in the home. It just wasn't. So we both privately blamed ourselves when Jeff got into some trouble in high school. In between blaming each other, that is. Until that one afternoon Jeff couldn't stand the accusations flying anymore and stood head to head with us and told us what was what. Told us what he really thought. Told us the truth, from where he sat. Did that ever hurt.

Strange. That was the first and only time Jeff ever confronted his dad and me about the choices we had made in life. Truth was, it didn't take but that one time. We were so shocked, we paid attention. More important, we started to change. Slow, toddling baby-step changes. But over time Jeffrey and I realized we'd given up too early. Should never had called it quits at all. But where could we go from here?

We started over. Began to date again. To talk and listen and forgive. To rebuild respect and trust. We did it. We planned on getting remarried. But then life did what it's so good at doing. Threw us a curveball we never expected. In a word. Cancer. Jeffrey was diagnosed in April and died in October. Once again, I felt like life was handing me too much, too soon. All that promise, mixed in with the grief. And after the grieving, regret took over. How I rehashed those lost years living as a single mom, struggling to make ends meet. Fighting to create some semblance of order and maintain a house, a home, for Jeff and myself. I was always weary. That life, those years, exhausted me. And just when I thought I had been given another chance by God, Jeffrey tells me he loves me—and then he died.

I was so hopeful. So expectant. Jeffrey and I held onto the promise that we could make up for those years when we were more concerned about getting our own way than with pleasing the Lord. Yes, we held onto hope that He would make up the difference just as we held hands through those blissful evening hours making plans for the future.

So now, today, what do I do? Isobel paused mid-thought. In her heart of hearts, God had already whispered the answer. Trust Me. That was it. Just as Jeffrey had tried to console and comfort Isobel before he passed away, God was stepping into her heart and mind urging Isobel to grasp hold of His grace through faith. Latch onto the Almighty's strength and not let go. Ever.

Consider family relationships the best "life" insurance policy you'll ever invest in. The dividends, the returns, are well above and beyond the cost.

So many emotions, Isobel thought. How can I make sense of them all? Sort them out right? Closing her eyes, Isobel prayed that God would give her that greater measure of faith to trust Him with her broken heart, every lost dream. That God would take the place of Jeffrey in her heart, that He would husband her from now on. She asked her merciful heavenly father for a fresh perspective that saw opportunities, possibilities, and—above all—would embody gratitude for today's new gift of life. For Kylie and for all the wondrous occasions she would have to love, and serve, and invest in her granddaughter's life.

Ready, Set, Adjust!

🌀 *Refuse to allow parenting mistakes to short-circuit the "grand" grandparenting opportunity.* Elyse was so excited about her daughter Lauren's pregnancy. She went on a shopping spree, buying everything she could conceive a baby would require. When she got home with all her purchases, Elyse phoned Lauren with the news, sure she'd be over-the-top thrilled with Elyse's purchases. Not. Elyse ended the call feeling not at all excited, or thrilled, or any other remotely happy emotion. No, Elyse felt humbled, chastised, and rebuked. Her daughter, kindly but firmly, reminded Elyse that they weren't taking any road that even slightly resembled the one Lauren had experienced as a child. If Elyse was honest with herself, she knew she was a controlling, hovering-over-every-detail kind of mom. And Lauren hated it. She talked with Elyse about this automatic take-control behavior even before she got married. Elyse always meant well, she really did. But she also needed to let go of control and allow her grown daughter to decide what was best for the baby—without falling into an emotional funk or responding badly by withdrawing altogether. Despite their volatile past history, mother and daughter would learn to parent and grandparent in a way that worked for both of them. In grand style.

※ *Cultivate hopefulness by identifying lessons learned from past shortfalls.* Fran had been abused as a little girl. She fought hard to work through those terrifying and frequently despair-filled memories. As she parented her own children, she realized that it was sometimes difficult for her to engage them emotionally. It seemed as though she was always fighting down her fears. Fran grew so much during her children's growing up years—she grew as much as they did, she believed. But sometimes when she looked back, it seemed as if she could not help feeling regret that she had not been more mature, more robust and stronger for her kids early on. Putting these thoughts aside, Fran chose to affirm how far she had come in the last twenty years. This gave her hope. And more reason than ever before to rejoice when she first heard her daughter's news that she was expecting a baby. This child, Fran determined, will always, always know she is loved and protected.

※ *Make prayer your highest priority in grandparenting.* Jody lived across country from both of her children and their families. While it didn't seem so bad when her kids first moved away and got married, now it was torture. Why? In a word. Grandchildren. Jody often felt like she was living on another planet so seldom were they able to visit. After lamenting this long-distance grandparenting business, Jody got down to business. If I can't be there in person, I can do one better, she realized. I can pray and pray and pray some more. There's no reason, no excuse, for me not to invest in my grandchildren's lives through the most powerful means given to me by God. And to let them know how much I love them, I'll email each one weekly prayer updates on what I'm specifically calling upon God to do in their lives and for them!

※ *Remember small kindnesses never go unnoticed.* Whenever Julie was home for the day, she cooked and baked and literally basked in the time spent in her kitchen. After her son and his wife had their twins, Julie noticed they were hitting the fast-food restaurants with alarming frequency out of energy deprivation. Just then, Julie had a little epiphany: why not double my recipes to help lighten their load? Why not indeed? Today Julie buys twice the amount of groceries required for her soups, casseroles, and baked goods. Then, she lovingly freezes the extras for her son and his family. Who knew that doing what Julie loves most to do would grow into a "double-blessing" when she put herself in her family's weary-worn shoes.

※ *Don't limit "gift" to financial support alone: give yourself away.* Nikki worked full-time at a doctor's office, scheduling patient appointments. On the weekends, Nikki considered Saturday her time to catch up on cleaning, shopping, and paying bills. Living on a tight budget, Nikki felt deep sadness that she wasn't able to give more to her four grandchildren by way of material gifts. Time was also in short supply. Then, Nikki decided that one weekday evening, the same day each week, she would offer to babysit her grandchildren for a few hours. It would be a standing invitation. She would make sure she had an easy dinner prepped ahead of time so she could concentrate on enjoying her grandchildren's company. What a hit! Nikki was surprised and gratified that almost every week all four of her grandchildren are dropped off for the evening by their folks. And what fun they have eating, playing simple games, just laughing together. And the cost? A little organization and a lot of love.

☀ *Schedule time to lighten the parents' load regularly.* Sara was a cleaning whiz. She always appreciated a quick walk-through of her home after she finished scrubbing, polishing, and sweeping. It was her vocation too. Sara knew all the tricks to swiftly work through a dirty, disorganized home and make it look sparkling . . . even inviting. Though Sara's grown daughters didn't need a babysitter much since their children were so busy with after-school sports, Sara wondered how to help her girls out more. She happened upon the perfect solution one day when she heard her oldest daughter say that she is so tired after working during the day and running in the evenings that she just doesn't have time to keep up with the housework. Perfect. While I don't want to take over their responsibilities, Sara thought, I can help out some. Once or twice a month I'll offer to come over and clean with my girls. Two hands . . . or four . . . make light work, right?

☀ *Don't give advice; give support, understanding, and encouragement.* Grace had to bite her tongue . . . literally. She didn't want to appear bossy or like a know-it-all. But goodness . . . she did know. She did! Grace had already walked this very road her daughter was now haphazardly beginning. Grace felt the hurt, endured the pressure, and still felt the painful repercussions of not listening to her ex-husband's opinion on discipline when they were still married. How Grace would love to turn back the clock and re-do some of her worst, most damaging parental missteps. But this cannot be. So now, Grace cringes when she sees her daughter being so capricious and lackadaisical in parenting her own children. She knows the storms that are sure to hit once her grandson becomes a teen. She won't listen to me, Grace thought, but I can pray. Pray that she'll learn from my errors ... and just maybe God will open up an opportunity for me to give some small bits of understanding and encouragement from a mom who learned the hard way.

 Be optimistically realistic by understanding your limitations as a grandparent. When Anna's stepdaughter got pregnant at sixteen, Anna's heart cried bitter tears. Having given birth to her own son at the tender age of seventeen, an unmarried, briefly-married, then soon-divorced Anna knew what her stepdaughter was facing. It hurt Anna to think about it. And yet, Anna remembered how her own mother had suffered right along with her, loving her and her child, supporting her through the rough times. It meant the world to Anna to have her mom's unconditional love. Even though it will bring back painful memories, she knows her stepdaughter will need the same kind of fierce love her own mother bestowed on her and her unborn child. Lord, help me to do what I can to practically help my stepdaughter and then trust You to make up the difference.

☼

Every Mother's Prayer

Lord,
Before you I stand, open-hearted, vulnerable, and so very aware of my past failures. As I close my eyes, all my shortcomings parade before me. They are enough to make me want to hide in shame. My lack of wisdom, my lack of caring, yes, my "lack" looms large before me. I wonder at your faithful, forgiving love toward me. After all I've done. The mistakes I've made, and will surely continue to make, in the future.

It amazes me that you call me out of a dismal past into a promising tomorrow. Lord, the regret I feel paralyzes me. So many lost opportunities. So many words left unsaid, or uttered for my own selfish gain. I'm ashamed at what I deemed more important than the people you gave me to love . . . and serve. How shortsighted I was. Still am, at times. But this I know, I have learned some lessons through the fires of my own making. And I purpose to make my family, my grandchildren in particular, my highest priority in life. Lord, help me to love and teach and guide these tender hearts toward you. Keep me focused on what's really important in life. People. My people. Help me, Lord, to be your ambassador of unconditional love to these fragile souls. Grow me up, Lord, so I can be worthy of being part of my grandchildren's growing up years as well. Thank you for giving me another chance to love in your name. Amen.

Thought for the Day

"God sends unfinished people to unfinished people with the message of his grace so that he can reclaim every heart for his glory."

—*Instruments in the Redeemer's Hands: People in Need of Change Helping People in Need of Change,* by Paul David Tripp

Chapter Nine

Negotiating the Convergent Life
The Struggle of Caring for Your Aging Parents

> *"If you serve, you should do so with the*
> *strength God provides, so that in all things*
> *God may be praised through Jesus Christ."*
> 1 Peter 4:11b

*E*ver notice that the more we hoard our time the quicker it seems to take flight? Interruptions give rise to anger, irritation, and the like. The stingier we become with our hours, minutes, and seconds, the further behind we get. It's a basic life truism that whatever is grasped is eventually rendered ineffective, unsatisfying, or altogether destroyed. While responsibilities loom large, deadlines threaten, and the workload seems to increase exponentially with each tick of the clock, the urgency of the day gives rise to ever-rising internal combustion. Likewise, this inmost orientation of the mind also produces a scarcity of generosity in spirit.

Study those rare individuals who are generous with their time, whose outlook is consistently "looking out" for others. Conversely, those whose vision of what is "time-worthy" is only as encompassing as the next item on their agenda eventually find themselves trapped in an ever-shrinking, despoiled environment. For these skinflintish (often productive, but frequently purposeless) souls there is never enough to go around, of time or anything else for that matter, and they pay dearly for hoarding. In this self-imposed prison of spirit, life erodes into an endless pattern of musts, have-tos, and imperatives that never allow the luxury of interruptions. Rigidity takes precedence over paying attention, and in paying attention to those around us—their needs, wants, and cares—we diminish ourselves, becoming people who miss the opportunity to see the value of interruption as the vehicle to some of life's most fulfilling surprises.

Study those rare individuals who are generous with their time, whose outlook is consistently "looking out" for others.

It is in the recognition that a day seldom passes that our schedules are not overridden by someone else's needs, demands, or desires, that we discover what side of the time clock we will position ourselves. Our task then (if our goal is to become the most efficacious of time stewards), becomes one of embracing a spirit generous with flexibility, offset with an extra measure of graciousness of heart.

When Pam's son died two years ago, she wanted to die with him. It was a sudden tragic death, a car accident no one could see coming. His death blindsided Pam in a way that even the death of her spouse had not. What is it about the bond between mothers and their children? Pam never gave it too much thought before, and now, even two years after her son's passing, she thinks almost constantly about that invisible bond that extends beyond this life and into the next.

Pam's son left behind a wife and two daughters, two beloved grandchildren for Pam to cherish and treasure. While Pam had always been a confirmed doting grandma, after Harv's death she planned her hours and days around spending as much time as possible with her granddaughters. In part, because she remembered how difficult it had been to parent solo after her own husband died when Harv was a teen. Also, because she now felt the frailty of life in a way she had never experienced before. True enough, Pam had dealt with loss, extreme sorrow, and had grieved sorely when her husband died. But she never, *ever* expected to outlive her precious son. That wasn't the natural order of things.

But it had happened, and now Pam was left with a loving daughter-in-law and two granddaughters to care for and support. She was thankful for the good relationship she enjoyed with her late son's wife. And Pam knew Casey so appreciated it when Pam dropped off meals midweek or stopped by with small gifts for the girls. It gave Casey a bit more time to rest and an emotional reprieve from being "mom" 24/7.

There was only one glitch in the system. Pam's parents. Never having been super close to her stoic, distant mother and father, Pam chose a completely different life path when she married her husband and raised Harv. Pam's own home was effusive with love and outward expressions of emotion. Having so craved even a single affirming word or a pat on the back during her own upbringing, Pam decided to create a home filled with love. She wanted her husband and her son never to doubt how she cherished them both. In this, Pam had succeeded marvelously.

Our task . . . becomes one of embracing a spirit generous with flexibility, offset with an extra measure of graciousness of heart.

What Pam had missed in her young years, she more than made up for with her own family and close friends. Pam's life was full and she was so very grateful for that. And yet, despite her blessings, Pam increasingly found herself becoming resentful toward her mom and dad. When the phone identified their number, more times than not Pam wanted to ignore the call. She didn't . . . mostly . . . but she was tempted. Her thoughts immediately ran along the lines of, "What could they want now? I just shopped and carted them around all afternoon two days ago." She knew it wasn't healthy or productive or honoring to the Lord . . . all these internal hesitations and emotional constraints.

But now, with Harv gone, Pam felt there simply wasn't time to care for both her parents (which she felt obligated to do) and her granddaughters (which she longed to do). What to do?

There wasn't a simple answer, at least none Pam could easily discern. Try as she might, as the weeks and months progressed Pam's resentment toward her parents' intrusion into her time and life continued to grow, as did her uneasiness about how she felt. So one day Pam decided to call a good friend who had been caring for her own elderly parents for some ten years while rearing her own brood of three kids. She made a list of her concerns and thoughts and wrote them down. But in reality, Pam didn't need the list; once they began talking, the two women covered every possible issue that arises when caring for two generations at the same time.

Her friend commiserated with Pam's feelings of resentment and admitted she felt the very same way at the beginning. Even now, all these years later, there are still crunch moments when Pam's friend struggles with the heavy load—the time deficit and the expectations from two sometimes not-so-grateful parents who have come to rely on her for everything. Pam breathed a huge sigh of relief just knowing this dear friend, a respected friend, had thoughts and feelings similar to her own.

Once they exhausted discussion of all the emotional challenges of care giving, Pam's friend helped her map out time in her weekly calendar that seemed reasonable for meeting both her parents' needs and her granddaughters' care. Seeing it in black and white brought still more comfort to Pam. She could see that she had been wasting more time than she realized, and her friend helped her learn to multitask when shopping and preparing meals: do it a single time for both sets of family . . . it will save you steps and energy. Sounded like a plan.

Lastly, Pam shared with her friend her desire to travel to Africa to begin a project in memory to her son. Pam's long-term goal was to search out a village in Africa where running water did not exist and help pay for several wells to be built as a memorial to Harv. Life to life—that's how Pam saw it. Her son would much rather have money spent on ensuring a healthy life for others than having a monument in a cemetery erected in his memory. So Pam and her friend discussed how Pam could get away for several weeks by enlisting some help from her friends to look in on her parents and by scheduling professionals to do what her friends couldn't. Pam's spirits lifted. She hadn't realized how heavy her heart had become, not only from the constant drain of care giving, but also from secretly fearing her dream for Harv's memorial would never come to pass.

Pam's friend gave her both practical and timely advice. She felt so thankful for their time together. The circumstances had not changed, but she now viewed them with a more hopeful, faith-inspired eye. She would be okay . . . and her parents would be fine . . . and her granddaughters would flourish as well. Pam felt secure that—one day at a time—she would be given all she needed for each and every day . . . from above . . . and that was more than she could ever ask.

Ready, Set, Adjust!

Spend time today squandering it for the sake of others. Grace was caught in a hard position. She still worked full-time, was the single mom of four teens, and had a sister who had been institutionalized as a young girl. Grace didn't have any other siblings, so when her dad lost his driver's license the year before, Grace took on the role of chauffeur as well, driving him wherever he needed to go. Never did she imagine that driving this one man around would add so many hours to her day. Grace really didn't mind. But after doing the necessary errands, she balked when he wanted to take a Saturday morning to drive out to visit her sister. After all, Grace visited her sister on her way home from work, and taking Dad would mean backtracking—an entirely new trip. After grousing for a few

Saturdays, Grace came up with a solution. She would enlist her four kids and the five of them would take turns on Saturdays driving Grandpa to see her sister. Grace even sweetened the deal for her kids. She gave them spending money for coffee and lunch after the visit. This way, everyone felt "treated" and special.

☀ *Lend your attention to someone in need of a listening ear.* With the phone in one hand and her other hand stirring a pot of chili, Melanie tried to remember how much chili powder she had already added to the mix. Ugh. Listening as intently as she could to her mom's detailed explanation of the morning's uneventful events, Melanie tried to remember if her mom had always been so detail oriented. She couldn't remember ever hearing this much inconsequential information before Dad died. So what happened to Mom's easy breezy ways? Dad died; now she's alone all day long and the little details she once shared with him are getting passed on to me, Melanie realized. Okay, I get it now . . . makes sense to me. If I were alone day in and day out, I would want to tell someone—anyone— about my thoughts too. Putting aside her concerns about the chili, Melanie sat herself down and began to really listen to her mom talk . . . and really, she found her mom's comments quite interesting.

☀ *Take a few moments to share in the interests of other people.* Anne never could figure out what her mom and dad liked about hummingbirds. But once they began to take on the snowbird mentality, traveling to either Florida or Arizona each winter, she started seeing hummingbird paraphernalia all around their home. Even spotted a kit for making a hummingbird feeder, a hummingbird magazine, and a curious recipe for the nectar these minuscule birds thrive on. While Anne didn't share their enthusiasm or understand it, she still encouraged it. Anne could see it was good for her parents' relationship to have something they were both so enthusiastic about. So she listened with rapt attention and slowly she grew to admire these tiny birds and their endearing ways almost as a way of saying thanks for enhancing her parents' compatibility.

☀ *Anticipate interruptions and determine to greet them as opportunities to expand in knowledge and life experience.* After Hannah received her eighth email from her dad that morning before lunch, she shook her head in utter amazement. It was cracking her up, this back-and-forth dialogue with her once so silent and uncommunicative father. Once he retired, all of a sudden he became computer savvy, learned how to use an iPod, even learned to text message Hannah's kids . . . which they thought was a hoot. Hannah worked out of her home, and her dad reveled in sharing each and every newfound tidbit of electronic know-how with her—all through the day. At first Hannah was a bit put-off by the interruptions, but now she views them as mini-breaks. Her dad doesn't need a whole page of response . . . it makes him happy just to pass on the information and know Hannah has received it. Information received, dad, and appreciated.

☀ *Focus on the larger scope of life by enlarging former perceptions of what qualifies as time-worthy.* Julie was far too goal and task oriented for her own mental health. Always had been. And whose fault is that? It's yours, Mom and Dad. You pushed me to achieve, achieve, achieve. And I did. And you were proud and pleased. But now you're both retired and all of a sudden you have time on your hands—time you want to spend with me—but I don't have that luxury. I'm still working, working, working. And you're seeing that the fruit of your parental labors might just be a little off-kilter. Julie ran that mental litany round and round her brain more times than she could count. But somehow, blaming her parents for the values they instilled in her when she was young didn't sit so well now. Julie realized as an adult she needed to rethink her parents' earlier out-of-balance parenting messages, and learn to pace herself not according to work standards but by building people into the grid as well.

✦ *Give precedence to the people around you, and demonstrate this by refusing to give in to impatient distraction.* Kim drove to her mom's house on the way home from babysitting her grandson for the day. He was still running a fever, still fussy, and her daughter was still debating about taking him to see the pediatrician. Kim hoped she would. Even if it turned out to be nothing more than a mild virus, Kim felt super-protective of her little grandson—maybe even more than she did her own daughter when she was a child. What's with that? Kim wondered. Pulling into the driveway, Kim was still feeling mightily distracted. But she had promised her mom she would bring over the newest family photos and discuss the upcoming holiday gatherings with her. It was a simple request, but Kim felt so torn and tired. So she offered a brief prayer for the Lord to help her put aside grandma-type concerns and give herself and her attention 100 percent to her mom who had always offered Kim the same consideration.

✦ *Cultivate the attitude that serving another person is always the highest privilege.* Sally was the youngest of ten, so her mom was more like a grandmother than a mother to her. When Sally was growing up, her older sisters did more mothering than her mom did. With such a large family, Sally often got passed around from one sibling to the next in her early years . . . and she loved it. Sally never felt slighted, but rather, adored, treasured, and so loved. Today, visiting her mom in the nursing home, Sally felt a sense of timeless wonder rush over her. She realized her mom would likely not live out the year, and Sally wanted above all to let her mom know in all the important little ways how much she loved her and appreciated the home her mom had made for them all. This is a real honor . . . giving back, isn't it, Lord? Thank you for the opportunity . . . not everyone gets to say thanks.

☀ *Recognize that God is the redeemer of all time and trust Him to make the most of your every moment.* With her own knee surgery scheduled just two weeks away, Cindy was trying to take care of both her family's and her parents' needs. Only two weeks from now, Cindy thought to herself, I'll be laid up for a while; there's so much to do. Feeling a rise of panic inside, Cindy took herself firmly in hand. Stop it, she told herself. Settle down. Make your list. And trust that God will give you the time and energy to do what needs to be done. And what doesn't get done . . . well, it just doesn't get done. Life isn't going to stop just because there aren't gourmet meals in the freezer and the kitchen floor hasn't been waxed. Get over it. So Cindy did. She slowly, and with deliberation, made herself a cup of tea, looked out the window, admired the lovely signs of spring approaching, and then made her to-do list much shorter than she had planned.

Every Mother's Prayer

Lord,
Today, I admit to feeling overwhelmed by the tasks before me. It is a constant struggle between what I desire to do with my time and what is necessary. It's not that I don't want to help and serve those in my care. The truth is, I feel torn, and so weary. Seems there are not enough hours in my day to satisfy everyone's wants. Perhaps I need to learn to see my life through fresh eyes. Certainly, I never anticipated that the second half of my life would be so encumbered with emotional pain and loss. Actually, I was hoping things would get easier as time went on. My family grown would mean more time for my plans. Or so I thought. But it hasn't worked that way. Always, always there is someone who needs my time and attention. Perhaps this isn't so bad? Just maybe I've been eyeing a future for myself that no one should covet. For surely if all my private desires and dreams

really came to pass . . . I would be alone . . . and lonely. Can't have it both ways. Either I choose this time of life to invest in me or I choose to invest in others. Really, there is no choice. Lord, help me today to cultivate an expansive, hopeful, grateful outlook, for it is always a privilege to serve another person. By your own example, You came to serve. Let my life emulate yours. Amen.

Thought for the Day

"We often hear people talk about the 'victorious Christian life.' But isn't the life of a Christian really more about bending the knee, humbling ourselves, and taking up a cross? Jesus said it is. 'If any of you wants to be my follower, you must put aside your selfish ambition, shoulder your cross, and follow me' (Matthew 16:24). I don't know what a cross will look like for you. I just know it will require a death to your desires and your dreams to carry it. And I know it won't be easy."

—*Holding On To Hope: A Pathway Through Suffering to the Heart of God,* by Nancy Guthrie

Chapter Ten

Pondering Remarriage
The Ongoing Dilemma of Beginning Again

The LORD's unfailing love surrounds
those who trust in him.
Psalm 32:10

What mother doesn't welcome those supportive "can do" or "I promise you" sentiments from valued friends and romantic prospects? Every one of us is bolstered by a good word. Or a good relationship. When those we count as respected peers recommend us to their contemporaries within the professional or the private sector, we inwardly rejoice. We are loved. We are wanted. We are . . . of worth. Not that we voice these sentiments aloud. Still, being considered *worthy* resonates powerfully with men and women alike.

Problem is, this need for acceptance frequently runs counter to more weighty and lasting considerations. Within the frame of something deeper, every single woman must ask what it is she most desires. Where will the "want" go? How far will women wander from ideals, worldviews, and faith, in order to gain another's good opinion or to attain the promise of a permanent relationship? Generally, the difficult choice is the right one . . . from just about any angle, in any circumstance, from anyone's vantage point. Saying no to sudden (or lingering) impulses can be heady stuff. Refusing to follow when every warm body around you is rushing herd-like ahead requires self-control and a good measure of personal integrity. These qualities aren't ones that rise to the surface in the heat of the moment; rather, they're nurtured and honed during the ups and downs of uneventful daily living.

When women "go for it" regardless of the cost to us or to others around us, through the ripple effect or by mere association with us, we're missing the whole point. Compromising and giving in to counterfeit shadow glories (frequently disguised as romantic companionship) yields nothing good. Sure, there are times when tough decisions must be made, and individuals may at times appear to be making brutal choices . . . in the short run. But when one takes a broader view of life, giving in to immediate gratification rarely proves to be wise. We mothers teach our children to forgo the trip to the candy store in favor of saving for a larger, more worthy purchase. Friends encourage friends not to give up during seasons of lingering illness or setback. Employers cast a vision for employees of what can be accomplished through hour by hour sacrifice. The common thread is embracing long-term vision and then working out the details to achieve one's goals day by day. Each day, every hour, no matter what the personal cost of time, energy, or self-sacrifice, people make choices that often have long-term consequences.

Refusing to follow when every warm body around you is rushing herd-like ahead requires self-control and a good measure of personal integrity.

The bottom line is this: when someone or something comes along and offers a shortcut, a detour, or an easy way out, beware. Better yet, "be aware." Stop, think, consider. In light of everything you believe in, does this current relational choice fit with the legacy you hope to leave behind? A reputation, like an honorable life, is indeed a precarious commodity . . . handle with care. Whether we moms like it or not, other eyes are upon us, waiting, watching, hoping we choose well.

Margie couldn't believe it. Here she was, fifty-three years old, crying in a movie theater . . . and not such a great movie at that. Trying to choke back her tears, they continued unbidden. What is with me? Margie wondered. She never cried like this. And never, ever in public. Her friend Kim didn't appear to notice the downpour . . . thank goodness for the darkness surrounding her. Fortunately Margie managed to compose herself and when the movie ended, a quick trip to the ladies room assured Margie that her makeup wasn't streaming down her face in murky mascara rivulets. Walking to their cars, Margie and Kim said their good-byes and parted ways. Driving home, Margie couldn't shake her convoluted emotions. Just what did happen back there? she asked herself for the umpteenth time. I can't believe I just fell apart over a movie . . . that movie! At a stoplight Margie tilted her head back, closed her eyes, and prayed momentarily for some insight, some wisdom. I don't like feeling this way, she stated aloud. I'm fine, Margie assured herself, just a momentary glitch in the system. Must be hormones. Better check my calendar. Or maybe it's the weather . . . storm brewing? Disgusted and confused, Margie drove the rest of the way home nursing her quiet despair in frustrated confusion.

Unable to sluff off her bleak feelings, Margie entered her house with a dark foreboding. She unlocked her door, flipped on the entryway light, and stood there. Gazing around her beautifully decorated living room, Margie had never felt so alone in her entire life. This is even worse than when my ex walked out the door, she thought morosely. Back then, I still had the kids with me. Alone. I am alone. I hate this.

Tossing her coat and purse onto the nearest chair, Margie went into the kitchen to check her messages. Nothing. Not a single one. See, she thought ruefully, that proves it, I am alone and no one cares. I could die tonight and who would ever know? No one. I hate this.

Margie continued to putter around her house, perfunctorily accomplishing inconsequential household tasks. Moving around, even this sort of mindless activity was better than sitting still and again replaying the evening's meltdown. By 11:00 p.m., Margie was worn out and headed to bed. Lying in the stillness, all those uncomfortable niggling thoughts came racing back into the fore-front of her mind.

Rehearsing the day, Margie told herself it was just because she was so tired. After all, she had worked a ten-hour day, driven straight to the restaurant to meet Kim and then see the movie. That movie—that horrible, despicable, stupid romantic comedy. Why did I ever agree to go to that one? Because normally it wouldn't faze you, Margie reminded herself. But today, you're not feeling normal. What exactly am I feeling?

Each day, every hour, no matter what the personal cost of time, energy, or self-sacrifice, people make choices that often have long-term consequences.

Angry, frustrated, disappointed, disillusioned, cheated. You name it, I'm feeling it . . . passionately. Margie turned the bedside light back on, sat up, and took her journal from the nightstand. Opening it, she started reading entries from several years earlier. Wow . . . I sure was angry then! And depressed and so discontent. Margie kept reading, stopping on this page or that to pause and really remember what those early days after her divorce had been like. Ink-black. That described it. And hollow. I was hollow inside. Hurting so much I couldn't feel a thing. But when the feelings came back, did they ever—non-stop roiling waves of such intensity I didn't think I would survive the next hour, let alone a whole day.

Tearing up, Margie continued turning page after page. Then she started to feel a tad lighter, maybe even a wisp of hopefulness. In her mind she was walking the hardest road she had ever walked all over again. But she had not been alone. God was with her. He promised to never leave or forsake her . . . and He hadn't. Margie managed a small smile. He—God—helped her . . . loved her . . . walked with her. I know it, Margie said aloud. Here, in black and white, I see how He came through for me every time I needed Him. Amazing.

Well, Lord, I need you again now, Margie whispered, I need You to help me sort through all these emotions I'm experiencing. You know me; You know that most of the time I'm really fine with living single. I am. What triggered all this upheaval in my heart tonight, I'm really not sure. But, will you help me understand my heart better? Help me give my disappointments and pain over to You again? I really am content with my life, aren't I? Maybe it's just the sappy way society portrays love that has me so worked up. What I saw on the big screen tonight is just not true . . . this romantic counterfeit to genuine self-sacrificing, hard-working, dying-to-self love. And it made my stomach ache. Real life, real love, doesn't even compare to this flimsy fantasy. Help me, Lord, to focus all my expectations and hopes on You alone. Trusting that if You want me to remarry, in Your day and Your time, You'll do the orchestrating as I live my life day by day. One last thought, Lord, by Your grace I've endured the brokenness of failed love; next time—if there is a next time—don't let me settle for less than the genuine article.

Ready, Set, Adjust!

Ask yourself, will today's action set me farther ahead or farther back? A close friend and co-worker of Candace's set her up for a date, a sailing outing to be precise. Candace couldn't believe how much fun she had. So the group planned a follow-up sail for the upcoming weekend. There was just one thing. A minor snag. Candace knew from her friend that her date, Tim, was not interested in working toward any sort of permanent relationship. I'm okay with that, Candace told herself. Or am I? Today, I'm fine with just being a social acquaintance, but what about next week, or next month? The longer I get to know this guy, would I still be fine with "just friends"? I don't think so, Candace admitted ruefully. I do want to be open to whatever God has in store for me, single or remarried, but it wouldn't be honest of me to start a relationship with this man, fully intending to "see where it goes," if he's made it just as clear he doesn't want to ever work toward marriage. Sure, today's fun might be pretty wonderful, but I don't want to invite disappointment or a broken heart by starting a no-future relationship.

✸ *Will I embarrass others or myself in making this choice?* I have my reputation to consider, Dorothy reminded herself. Again. So why don't I just call it off right this very minute? she wondered. Because I'm in the throes of an emotional crush . . . at my age even. It's embarrassing. Still, I am not seeing any indications that my life is headed in the same direction as my gentleman friend. And why do I feel myself blushing when my kids ask about him? They think I don't see the warning signs. Married and divorced three times already . . . do I really think I'll be the one to reform him? I suppose, in my more desperate moments I do believe that. But in the light of day, I know better. I've already lived through the pain of being widowed after loving a very good man. I don't want to throw away that wonderful legacy and memory by settling for less than best now. Lord, help me get my head on straight and break off this "going nowhere fast" relationship today.

✸ *Can I defend my decision morally?* All her friends were going, why shouldn't she go too? Renting that huge beach house sounded like a dream come true after weeks of deadlines and overtime and weekends spent on-call. Rita really wanted to go, but she couldn't quite get past the fact that everyone was pairing up, sharing bedrooms, and none of them were married. Okay. Well, not okay. Rita was not okay with this arrangement, not sure her boyfriend was either. She would have to tell her friend who was organizing the trip that she couldn't go if she wasn't able to have her own room. Rita already knew what kind of uproar her stand would cause. Oh well. It's not the first time, and probably won't be the last. But at the least, I'll be sleeping with a clean conscience.

☀ *How far-reaching are the repercussions?* Jan's two daughters were now in college at a local university and she was amazed at how much her time had been freed up in the past year. No longer was she planning meals for three; it was takeout for one or tossing a salad together most evenings. It was during one of those solitary meals that Jan started thinking about her future. She had some land she had purchased years earlier, before the market skyrocketed. She thought about selling her home and moving up north, building a new home, and settling in near the lake for good. All that quiet sounded pretty appealing—maybe when she was eighty! Then Jan thought of a better plan. She really had the itch to open a coffee bar. She had owned, run, and sold several other businesses, so she knew what she was doing. Knew what it cost too. And yet, Jan felt compelled by this back-burner notion. The more she ruminated over the idea, the more details seemed to fall into place. I'm not married, not dating, I've got two daughters who are almost on their own, what better time than now to pursue my dream? If I sell my land, I'll have the capital to open my own shop. This was not the first time Jan was grateful for her singleness . . . pleased and content that she could follow her personal dream without having to consult with and concede to someone's else's long-term goals. It wasn't always so rosy being a single mom, but on certain days it did have its perks.

☀ *How does my past affect the way I view romantic possibilities today?* Was she still that wounded? Bitter? Angry? Resentful? Marlene tried to answer that question honestly. Every one of those hurtful words had been lobbed at her by her present fiancé. And she wondered. Was it true? Marlene viewed herself as realistically as she knew how. She was aware that the pain and hurt she experienced from being "left" by her former spouse had affected her. Big time. Still, hadn't she worked through all that heartache in the years since he exited? Marlene thought she did a pretty good job of moving forward. And yet, Marlene recognized some small truth in her fiancé's comments. She did tend to respond defensively, she did view men in general with skepticism, and she did find it difficult to accept her fiancé's love without holding back. Maybe, just maybe, I haven't moved along as far as I thought. Lord, help me see what's really going on in this heart of mine and help me change what needs fixing.

✷ *Can I honestly be content living my life as a single woman?* Sitting in the car repair shop, Alyssa bemoaned to her best friend the lack of a live-in handyman in her life. Normally Alyssa, a newspaper journalist, relished her independence. Since her kids were grown and gone, she was free to pursue her career with a gusto those early parenting years prohibited. There was only one aspect to living single that made Alyssa think twice about growing old on her own. It was car repairs . . . car maintenance . . . even buying a car threw Alyssa into angst. As she sat there, observing incoming and outgoing traffic, she took note. Being the overzealous observer that she was, Alyssa noticed any number of women, with no ring on their left hand, getting their vehicles repaired. Somehow that insignificant fact made her feel better. Alyssa consoled herself with the fact that ninety percent of the time she was just fine with living as a single woman. And really, no one's fine all the time. Everyone, even married couples, need help from others.

✷ *In what way would remarrying change my parenting role?* Cassie was about to break the news to her adult son and daughter that she was now engaged. She didn't think it would be a big deal to either of her children. After all, she had been dating Mike for the past three years and the kids were fine with that. So after dinner one Sunday afternoon, Cassie was shocked when neither of her children offered any congratulatory remarks when she told them her plans. It was awkward and disappointing. Why can't they be happy for me? Cassie didn't say a whole lot more about the touchy subject, but in the following days she gave an inordinate amount of thought to it. She realized her kids were most likely afraid of a change that would "change" their relationship with her. What if Mike disagreed with the kids on something? How would they handle holidays, birthdays, and vacations? Would all their family traditions be discarded for new ones? These considerations gave Cassie pause. She now understood her children's reaction, or lack of it. We need to talk and the kids need to know that some things will change but my love for them isn't one of them.

❂ *Does this romantic relationship enhance or detract from an honorable legacy?* Bethany had a tough decision to make. She had fallen hard for a man who didn't share her faith. How could that have happened? Looking back, it occurred without her knowing it. Small courtesies, short but pleasant conversations that led to longer intimate sharing. Bethany wanted to scream. She knew better than to put herself in a situation like this, but it happened anyway. Bethany sighed. Okay, I made a huge blunder . . . one that involves my heart. What do I do now? Bethany didn't want to end this relationship. And yet, inside, she knew there wasn't any way she would marry a man who wasn't more in love with Christ than he was with her. Good for Bethany that she had two friends who talked sense into her, kept her accountable and on track. It wasn't easy to do, and it would hurt—a lot—but Bethany was old enough to understand that it is far wiser to endure temporary pain for a season than to compromise her standards and live a lifetime of regret.

Every Mother's Prayer

Lord,

My life story certainly didn't play out as I expected it. I envisioned a rosy married life, complete with assorted perfect children who never gave me a moment's worry. So much for my dreamy, unrealistic expectations. Still, though divorce became part of my life, it does not have to become my identity. I am, first and foremost, your child, Lord. I belong to You. Your Word says that You delight in me. Wonderful thought, worth remembering every hour. I am never alone, You are always with me. Your Word promises that too. You have a future filled with hope for me. Another pledge from the King of Kings. I'm in awe of how complete, and full, and defining Your love is for me. And yet, there are moments. You know them. When I feel unloved, alone, and so hopeless. I wonder if I'll ever have the opportunity to love in a romantic sense again. Maybe yes, maybe no. But this I do know. You, my Father God, will supply all my needs according to Your riches in glory. I count on it! By faith, I aim to please You by trusting in Your goodness and care for me. And I ask for a generous supply of wisdom and discernment so that I do not dishonor You in my choices. You know my fickleness and my frailty. Lord, put a hedge around me, close me in, and cover me with your vigilant love. Always, Lord, let me first look to You to fill me—heart and soul. Amen.

Thought for the Day

Jesus himself said, "I came so they can have real and eternal life, more and better life than they ever dreamed of" (John 10:10). Life instead of death. Hope instead of despair. Even joy in the midst of terrible sorrow. A new kind of living—harder, but better in some ways, than before. Maddening because we hate the process, but richer because of the pain. Life. Pure and simple. It's a choice. It's a new kind of normal."

—*A New Kind of Normal: Hope-Filled Choices When Life Turns Upside Down,* by Carol Kent

Chapter Eleven

Accepting the Limitations that Come with Aging

A Needed Reality Check

I can do all this through him
who gives me strength.
Philippians 4:13

Rest and work: how difficult it is to find (and maintain) that chronically elusive balance between these two competing positions. For many women, especially those high-achieving "all-together" ones, a generalized underlying feeling of self-induced accomplishment anxiety is so commonplace they often don't even recognize its existence. Until, that is, their bodies tell them otherwise. While it is natural to feel a racing pulse or a quickening of breath in moments of danger or fear, it is not normal to experience symptoms of anxiousness and physical upset the majority of the time. And yet, as we age our bodies' decreasing tolerance for overuse, abuse, and high stress is rarely taken into account. Women continually push, push, push, until something gets their attention long enough to stop them.

The physical danger alone to a woman whose body is on constant "high alert" can be both extensive and cumulative. Women who experience chronic irrational fears or dread, chest pain, muscle tension, headaches, heart palpitations, insomnia, GI distress, tearfulness, depression, and/or overall jumpiness should seek out medical care that addresses every aspect of our whole being—physical, emotional, and spiritual.

Clearly, it is our frenetic lifestyles that contribute and exacerbate this growing anxiety-related, expecting-too-much- from-ourselves epidemic. And single moms are among the worst offenders: having handled life at its very worst and succeeded despite the challenges before them, they now fail to allow themselves needed time for rejuvenation as they grow older. Even those rare women who do recognize their escalating need for increased regularly scheduled rest often miss the fuller biblical concept of purposeful, regular retreat from the daily grind, . . . which is more of an inner renewal than anything else and naturally lends itself to healthy introspection and more reasonable life expectations. Life is always in flux. It is never stagnant. What worked for a mom last year can overwhelm her this year. From every angle, during every season of life, the balance between rest and work is truly curative and biblically mandated.

While it is natural to feel a racing pulse or a quickening of breath in moments of danger or fear, it is not normal to experience symptoms of anxiousness and physical upset the majority of the time.

Taylor was covered in a web of sickening sweet, sticky, pink and blue sugary substance. It was in her hair, on her face, in her eyelashes, and now completely ingrained in the fabric of her clothing . . . Taylor was a living, breathing, cotton-candy-coated nightmare. After four hours of inhaling minuscule sugary granules and frantically spinning wispy colorful cotton candy cones for children of all ages, Taylor was exhausted. Her feet hurt. Her legs hurt. Her back hurt. So did her head. She was worn out. I can't ever remember feeling so drained after a church event before, she lamented to no one listening. This used to be fun.

Once home, Taylor plopped down on the first comfy couch she could reach and melted into it body and soul. Stretching out, she gave in to the temptation to take a brief early-evening nap and closed her eyes. Out. Like. A. Light.

Some forty-five minutes later she awoke, stiff and groggy, and feeling more "put-out" than before she slipped into slumber. Oh, why did I do that? she moaned. I know better than to nap in the evening, now I won't sleep tonight. Groaning, Taylor pulled herself up and plodded into the kitchen for a drink of water before going to wash off all the goop. I need a good soaking in a hot tub, she decided. So she did. Soak and rest. Wonderful.

Funny what a bath full of bubbles will do for you, Taylor mused, now that she was feeling relaxed and getting her second wind. Putting on her coziest pajamas and a pair of snugly socks, Taylor settled back to do some bill paying and then indulge in some just-for-fun reading before bed. Pulling out her checkbook, Taylor got busy writing checks and had one of those epiphany moments that stopped her cold. Thumbing through the checkbook pages, Taylor took note of where her money was going. More important, she noted where the bulk of her time was being spent. I can't believe this, she said out loud. Whoever said that looking through a person's checkbook reveals what that individual values most was sure right. And it isn't even about money. It's about my time. I'm getting a snapshot of my life just by skimming through my checkbook. Who would have thought?

From every angle, during every season of life, the balance between rest and work is truly curative and biblically mandated.

I'm too busy. How can one single woman be involved in all these different activities? And paying for them? I sure am paying for it, in more ways than I'd like to admit. Something has got to give. Taylor studied the past six months of transactions and shook her head in dismay. I'm overbooked. I've overspent. No wonder I feel like I have nothing left to give. Who am I kidding? I'm not twenty anymore. Not thirty. Or forty. I'm a fifty-something single mom who's spent the majority of my adult life working hard. At my job, for my kids, just to survive. But this isn't survival mode—this is just stupid!

You would think that now that my kids are grown, I would be allowing myself some time to recoup and recharge. It isn't so. Instead, I've done what? Foolishly signed up for every volunteer service activity that someone presents to me. Lord, help me! Show me how to untangle myself from these commitments, I simply cannot handle this pace any longer. Tonight proved it. What used to be fun and enjoyable has become a burden my body can no longer bear. I'm not as resilient as I once was and it takes me longer to gain back my strength after such strenuous physical labor.

Closing her checkbook, Taylor took out her calendar and address book. She started jotting down a new to-do list. But this list wasn't anything similar to Taylor's previous to-do reminders. No—just the opposite—she was making practical plans to begin "undoing" those unnecessary and life-draining tasks that were detracting from the life she knows God is calling her to live for Him. Taylor reminded herself that she has only one body, and she alone is responsible for caring for it. She then chided herself for so mindlessly saying yes when people tried to pressure her into joining yet another committee or service project.

No more. I know I won't be popular in some circles for putting a stop to this circus, but if I don't begin an immediate cease and desist action, my poor body will. Balance. Isn't that what I just preached to my daughter last week? No wonder she snickered at me. Taylor remembered the occasion with embarrassment. There I was, dusted over with confectioner's sugar from frosting six dozen cookies while playing phone tag with the chairperson for an overseas trip we're putting together. The telephone rang, my cell phone went off, and the doorbell chimed . . . and my daughter said, "Right Mom, it's all about balance!" And then she left with that "do as I say, not as I do" look on her face. Ouch.

All right, tomorrow, after a good night's sleep, I'm going to start disentangling myself from this web of over-commitment and I'll begin with a call of apology to my dear girl . . . and thank her for reminding me that I'm not above my own advice!

Ready, Set, Adjust!

 Understand the link between emotional and physical changes and PMS, perimenopause, and menopause. Yvonne's OB had given her notice about five years back. She ordered the blood work, listened to Yvonne's symptoms and pronounced judgment. Or what felt like judgment at the time: you're on the fast track to menopause, but I'm here to help. After a long discussion of what to expect and what to do about the changes occurring in her body, Yvonne left her doctor's office feeling hopeful; more important, she left feeling reassured that she was normal. You can't pay for that kind of comfort.

 Practice good nutrition. Eat whole foods and stay clear of caffeine, sugar, and simple carbohydrates ("white foods" are a woman's enemy). Shannon was a coffee fiend—loved it and lived for it. Sad, but true. Other women enjoyed a cup each morning at breakfast; Shannon wanted it mainlined into her system before getting out of bed. While Shannon was more careful about her diet, she still found herself falling into unhealthy patterns more and more frequently. One cookie led to six. A handful of potato chips begged for another handful. And her coffee habit . . . well, she admitted that was out of control. Still, Shannon didn't think it was that big a problem until she began having odd physical symptoms. Rushes of adrenaline complete with heart-racing anxiety attacks. She started wondering how much of these now daily reactions were diet induced? Shannon talked with other women her age and they told similar stories. No doubt, her body was talking to her. But would she listen?

✵ *Be physically active. Touted as the single best anti-anxiety medication, women should engage in moderate daily exercise.* Susan used to be a runner, for ten years she ran between four and five miles every day save Sunday. She loved it. Once she hit that one-and-a-half mile mark, Susan felt like she could run forever. Then she got married and had kids. Somewhere in between all her daily responsibilities, running—any exercise at all—took a back seat. Susan couldn't believe how quickly muscle turned to smoosh—that was her pet word for her now not-so-firm body. Off and on for years, Susan would begin an exercise regimen only to forsake it a few months later. Finally, after her divorce and after her kids grew up, Susan decided to try and drop that extra twenty pounds by getting her body back. She was increasingly irritable, anxious, and restless, and since she lived alone now, Susan couldn't blame those feelings on anyone else. No, it was her changing body that was sending out warning signs that sounded suspiciously like a manufacturer's owner's manual: no longer in use, out of date, and warranty expired. With every ache and pain, and additional pound, Susan felt chastised for taking better proactive care of her household appliances than she did of herself. And, Susan laughed, with me there isn't any money back guarantee!

✵ *Get enough sleep. Set up a nightly routine for bedtime and stick to it.* Women in general require seven to nine hours of sleep per night for better brain/body health. Trish was a night owl. While her co-workers talked about getting to bed early, she wondered, why? Trish never seemed to need much sleep; four to five hours a night and she felt refreshed. Unlike her peers, Trish got more accomplished after 11:00 p.m. than before. She loved the quietness of her home at night. Uninterrupted, Trish would steamroll ahead, ticking off her mental task list. It was what Trish did best. That is, until she had her hysterectomy. Trish couldn't quite figure out the physiological tie, but she was sure of one thing. Ever since that surgery, she was ready for bed come 10:00 p.m. Assuming it was due to post-operative recovery, Trish didn't think much of it at first. Now, a year later, Trish asked her physician more pointed questions. It's a mix, her doctor told Trish. Between your body adjusting to sudden menopause and aging itself; everything shifts. Get used to it, and listen to what your body is calling for. So Trish did. Now, no longer the night owl, she listens more closely to her co-workers as well, taking tips from them on how they manage their homes in the midst of the chaos.

☀ *Go outside for some sun exposure. Take fifteen minutes a day (without sunscreen) to encourage the production of Vitamin D that helps stave off mood disorders such as SAD.* Hannah had always and forever been an indoor kind of gal. Sort of ironic for this watercolor artist who specialized in painting floral and other natural wonders. Hannah would gather her tools and head outside in search of the most unique settings in her town. And she knew right where to go to locate those one-of-a-kind picturesque locales that had her buyers oohing and ahhing. Hannah was likewise a skilled photographer, which saved her stepping outdoors more than necessary come October through March. She would photograph all through the warmer seasons and paint indoors through the bone-chilling months. Hannah always thought this was a perfect setup. Until she started fighting bouts of depression in the bleak winter months. Nothing in her circumstances had changed, so why did she feel so blue? Hannah's good friend suggested it might be more physical than emotional. She probed a bit, and chastised her friend for not getting out more . . . and Hannah's friend meant "out" literally. You need the benefit of sunshine on your skin every day . . . every single day. So, bundle up and force yourself to walk outside no matter how much you'd prefer to stay indoors. Hannah decided that braving the cold might be easier than enduring those dark moods, so she made it her new habit to step outside . . . and further than her mail box . . . for a brisk twenty-minute walk around her neighborhood each afternoon. To her amazement, Hannah discovered there were winter scenes worth painting that were just waiting for her to discover them.

☼ *Take emotional inventory. Revisit current familial, work, and volunteer responsibilities, then make adjustments as warranted.* Over time, Gretchen had accumulated more than just "stuff" in her home and garage; this single mom of five just kept adding on more and more work-related stress to her load of life. As an ER nurse for over twenty-five years, Gretchen had seen it all and was keenly aware of how quickly people went over the edge. During her initial diagnostic questioning with a patient Gretchen could identify and remedy not only physical ailments, but the emotionally induced ones as well. Too bad it took her non-medically trained children and friends to identify and offer a remedy for her incessant habit toward overwork on every front. Resistant at first, Gretchen eventually took heed and stepped back for a clearer look at her life and its stresses. She certainly did not want to end up as a patient in the ER, and she had to admit that she was losing her empathy and her patience with the patients! Maybe that was the loudest signal of all.

☼ *Schedule regular time for rest. Then give these slotted time segments the priority they deserve.* When Martha took over as the school administrator's head secretary, she never realized how many hours she would be working into the evening. Martha considered it a step up, this new position, and true enough the pay increase made Martha sleep easier at night, knowing that retirement arrives sooner rather than later. But still Martha had days, weeks even, when she wondered if the money was worth it. Every evening now she went home exhausted and dreaded the alarm going off the following morning. Dragging herself into each day was no easy task. Martha lived for the weekends . . . not to enjoy them, but to sleep. Was it a mistake to take this new job? Martha admitted the answer was yes, though she hated the thought of having to talk to her boss about her struggles. But Martha knew herself well enough, knew what her body requires to stay healthy. Regular rest . . . and right now she wasn't getting enough, not of sleep and certainly not of downtime. It's only a matter of time, Martha admitted, before a larger force than me puts a halt to this pace.

 Research insurance benefits that may include age-related benefits. Nancy couldn't recall being more delighted. Imagine! Her insurance company paying for her weekly swim aerobic classes as part of their stay-well incentive. She could get into this. As a longtime budgeter out of necessity, Nancy never felt she had the extra money to put toward fitness clubs and classes. But with her firm joining an insurance company offering these incentives, Nancy wouldn't turn it down. Getting her cell phone out, she started calling all her friends too . . . wouldn't it be fun if we all got into the same classes together? Now that's what I call getting the most out of every dollar from my investment.

✷

Every Mother's Prayer

Lord,
Will you help me to be wise as I grow older? Prudent enough to know when to say enough is enough? Far too often I push myself too hard. Then, nothing turns out, or feels, right. I am undone in every way imaginable. And then I wonder why life is so hard. Most of the time, it's because I invite these stresses into my life. Too many

hours at work, volunteering, or serving my church, even helping with my family. I pray that You enable me to have the courage to say no when I have reached a reasonable limit of work each day. It does no one any good when I am overextended and irritable, when I become sick because of exhaustion, or when I feel depressed after having taken on more than my share of burdens.

Oh Lord, put a watch before my mind's eye . . . catch me, restrain me, before I fall headlong into more responsibility, activity, service than I can bear. Teach me to pace myself, instruct my heart in humility, for I often wrongly feel it's my responsibility to "do" for others when You want them to do for themselves. I thank You for my life, even my limitations in this aging body, for I know that as I seek You first, You will give me all I require to accomplish Your will for me today. Stay close by my side, and when I lapse into discouragement and weakness, shore me up with Your great arms of strength and encouragement. Let me learn what it means to rest in You. Let me learn what it means to commit my work to You, knowing that You alone measure success, and that by Your measure I must order my days. Amen.

Thought for the Day

"Do you desire to know the Lord more? Do you want to share in the rare depth of strength that comes straight from the throne room of heaven? This kind of strong grace doesn't come to those who don't need it. It's a precious gift for those who are weak and desperate. The Lord comforted Paul by telling him that His grace—and just His grace—was enough for him. Will it be enough for you?"

—*Will Medicine Stop the Pain? Finding God's Healing for Depression, Anxiety, & Other Troubling Emotions,* by Elyse Fitzpatrick and Laura Hendrickson, M.D.

Chapter Twelve

Discovering Joy and Contentment Despite the Unknown

The Unchanging Faithfulness of God

Not that I have already obtained all this, or have already arrived at my goal, but I press on to take hold of that for which Christ Jesus took hold of me. Brothers and sisters, I do not consider myself yet to have taken hold of it. But one thing I do: Forgetting what is behind and straining toward what is ahead, I press on toward the goal to win the prize for which God has called me heavenward in Christ Jesus.
Philippians 3:12–14

We are all storytellers. From earliest recollections, most of us can remember being read to from storybooks as young children. Some of these tales were funny, some sad, some were meant to impart a life lesson, others were just fun. But every one of them contributed to our worldview and helped develop our critical thinking process, either accurately or not so. What we women believe (or once believed) shapes our behavior and our thinking; it did then and continues to do so throughout our entire lives. Which is why it is so valuable to continue this practice of storytelling into adulthood. Unfortunately, many mothers don't give enough thought to how much impact they have on those around them (and vice versa) via sharing their stories. So they stop talking . . . about what matters, that is.

As single moms living in a high-tech society, it is so easy to become automatons. Self-reliant, self-sufficient, self-protective; to the nth degree we women have mastered the art of solo status . . . in ways that are the most costly. Sure, we live in families, we may share an office, attend neighborhood gatherings, yet simultaneously we remain apart. Only as people venture forth with prudent self-storytelling for the purpose of enriching someone else's life will others offer similar exchanges. It truly is a trust begets trust principle.

Counselors routinely sit opposite desperately hurting individuals who are simply in need of a listening, empathetic ear. Sadly, our society has placed such a premium on projecting the image and illusion of perfection that genuine self-disclosure is becoming a rare commodity indeed. Even within the church, especially within the church. For want of an ordinary "good word," many women are forced to make an appointment with a professional just to get a hearing. Not that counselors aren't needed, they are, but as fellow life travelers we women must consider how much we have to offer one another by merely living lives of honest transparency.

What we women believe (or once believed) shapes our behavior and our thinking; it did then and continues to do so throughout our entire lives.

Everyone struggles. Everyone bleeds. Everyone needs a good hand of help, a word of hope, and a renewed life perspective. As moms embrace the eternal by enlarging their own vision of what God can do, has done, only then can they become the conduit of substantive strength for their children, grandchildren, and every other person they are honored enough to influence. And in the very act of influencing for life, women will find their own vision for the future expanded and multiplied by God's gracious hand.

Christine and Marie and Ashley were three best friends. They had known each other since junior high and although they parted ways after high school, soon after college they all ended up back in their hometown. In so many ways their lives mirrored one another's. They all married. They each had children soon after tying the knot. All three opted out of the workforce when their kids were little. They talked and prayed and cheered each other on through every imaginable parenting and marital dilemma. They were best friends. They shared just about everything, each sorrow was divided, each happiness multiplied. It was the way life was supposed to work with the ones you love.

Then everything seemed to break all at once. Christine's husband left her. Followed by Marie's husband. And life didn't make so much sense anymore. Ashley cried buckets of tears for her two closest friends, wondering how it could have happened to such wonderful women. To her best friends! No one could fault either of these two dedicated and loving wives and moms. In truth, even their exes didn't fault them. Which made it almost worse. Christine and Marie were left second-guessing why their respective spouses ended the marriages if they didn't "do anything" to precipitate their exits.

Between the three of them they drank more coffee, ingested more chocolate, and consumed more boxes of tissues than any of them could calculate. That was at the beginning. A few months after the shock wore off, some of the intensity of the emotions began to fall off as well. Day by day, life went on, and they coped by having one another at their sides or patting their backs while commiserating together. When the divorces were finalized, the tears fell with a vengeance again. This time, however, those volatile likely-to-leave-you-crippled emotions didn't last quite so long before leveling off once more. The trio knew they had turned a significant corner when Ashley told of some half-comical but thoroughly aggravating marital incident and they all laughed uproariously, Christine and Marie simultaneously telling their friend "Better you than me (us!)" to Ashley.

So began the real healing, the next step in their new lives. That was the day all three recalled as the turning point. Hope. That's what it felt like . . . hope. If they were able to laugh again, then they could face living too. And like every other woman, married, divorced, or single . . . life keeps moving along. Christine and Marie rebuilt their lives as single moms. Ashley, still married, would regale them with true-to-life marital hardships . . . just to keep it real, she told them. And they would compare their lives . . . different yes, hard, true enough. Between the three of them, these women realized some important life lessons.

Sadly, our society has placed such a premium on projecting the image and illusion of perfection that genuine self-disclosure is becoming a rare commodity indeed.

First, life is hard. Period. Doesn't matter what your marital status is . . . and at times both Christine and Marie were very grateful they were living single. On other days, or under different circumstances, Ashley was the one who was grateful to be married. But each of them every day thanked God for their lives as they were; they knew He was in charge, at the forefront, and leading the way. Didn't matter what tomorrow would bring. Didn't matter if Christine and Marie never remarried. Didn't matter if Ashley's husband might die before her, leaving her on her own in old age. Didn't matter.

What did matter was that all three women learned that God's Word is faithful and true. His love is constant and never changing. God wasn't surprised on those perilous days long ago when Christine's husband and then Marie's decided to leave them and their children. God saw it all in advance and made preparations for them. He knew what they would feel and face, so he gave them a family . . . specifically, a family of friends. Three women who loved each other enough to stand by in the good times and carry each other through the bad. What a gift . . . each one to the others. And these women knew it. They weren't afraid of unknown tomorrows; they were too busy giving thanks for God's gift of today. And busy making plans to surprise each other with fresh ways to say "I love you, friend!"

Ready, Set, Adjust!

Step one: recognize the standards by which you live life. Review life patterns, current choices, and future aspirations. Lucy browsed through all the Sunday pre-holiday advertisements . . . with discontent. She saw lots of gifts she longed to buy her family, but didn't have the budget for it. Continuing to flip through the paper, this retired salesperson noticed an ad to which she felt suddenly tempted to respond. Lucy gave in against her better judgment. Next thing, Lucy didn't know which end was up . . . literally. She was hired as a holiday "extra" at the local mall and her job, which she chose to accept, was to restock the shelves in the middle of the night. Lucy, fit for her age, was excited about the chance to earn some needed Christmas money for those special gifts for her grandkids. So the second full week into her temporary job, Lucy was busy restocking the uppermost tier with toys—silly toys Lucy thought to herself—reaching higher yet . . . and then she fell. Good thing she had just started for the night, for she landed on a heap of plush squeeze stuffed animals that covered the hard floor beneath her . . . thank the good Lord. Lying there, Lucy's head spun . . . literally. Just why am I doing this again? Lucy grimaced as she shouldered herself up to a sitting position. What will the kids say? Bumped and bruised, and for what? A little extra cash! Goodness, when am I going to learn: I don't need extra money to show my family how much I love them. Didn't I learn a thing from overspending all those

years I had to work? Apparently not, and she tossed the nearest, newest, had-to-have toy away in exhausted frustration.
I'm losing sleep and perspective!

✦ *Step two: schedule time for reassessment.* Ask for input, ideas,
and observations from other women as to how they see you/
your life. Charice was happily seated around her dining room
table with her very favorite people . . . her book club friends.
This small group of ladies met every six weeks for in-depth discussion and friendly banter. They loved it. What started out as
an informal gathering between professional women grew into
mutually satisfying friendship characterized by trust. Charice
decided that she needed some wise advice. Her son had invited
her to move into the in-laws apartment attached to his family's
home. Should she or shouldn't she? Charice couldn't decide.
Listing the pros and cons didn't help. Both courses of action
had benefits and drawbacks. Maybe she was just too close to
the situation? What does a woman do when her mind's in a
muddle? She gets advice from those who know her best. So
that's what Charice did.

✦ *Step three: adopt a brutal slash/strike mentality to eliminate
any activity or task that promotes the notion that busy is
better.* Take on the less-is-more, minimalist's stance regard-
ing commitments. Rose had four sisters, all living, and it felt
more like she was their mother than their peer. All these long
adult years since their folks had died, Rose had been the plan-
ner, the executor of holidays, birthdays, and vacations. And
of course her sisters loved it. Sure they did. It meant they had
only to arrive on time with a dish or two, while Rose labored
to plan, prepare, and serve an ever-growing number of extended family members. One day in late October, just as she
normally did, Rose pulled out the yearly calendar and started
writing down potential dates for their family get-togethers
when her pen stopped working. How tiresome! Getting up
to find another, Rose stopped herself. Tiresome is right! I am

worn out. I think it's time for the five of us to start divvying up these gatherings equally, and if we can't agree on a date that works for all of us, then we'll skip it. Rose smiled. It will be good to be invited as a guest for a change!

✸ *Step four: appreciate today. Despite the angst and the irritations, learn to see and value every day as an opportunity to grow, to give, to be.* Helen was never the full-glass gal; from early on, she saw only what was missing. That is, until her entire life went missing—her husband died, kids left home, her brother and his wife moved south permanently. For all practical family purposes, Helen was alone and she finally felt the sting of so many years of fearfully hoarding what relationships God had given her. Sitting in her kitchen over her morning coffee, Helen knew she had a decision to make. Either she could bemoan everything she had lost, or . . . she could determine to give back. Helen decided right. She began giving back. As a retired single mom, Helen had many gifts. So she started volunteering at a nearby school, teaching the wives of foreign professionals how to speak and write English. Helen loved it. And through their many conversations, Helen found herself saying no to invitations to dinner and plays and even family birthdays. Not that she didn't want to go, but there were too many to attend! Helen gave of herself and gained.

✸ *Step five: let a spirit of gratitude spill over into every act, every hour, every day.* Annie prayed that the Lord would help her see, with His eyes, all the good that remained in her life. Annie was grateful, she was. But there were moments, like yesterday, when her daughter called from clear across the country and her three-year-old grandson got on the phone to say hello. It was wonderful. Until they hung up. Then Annie felt bereft and lonely. Lord, help me . . . to simply be grateful I have a daughter who loves me, and she's been given a dear little boy to love her. This is good, and I'm not going to allow self-pity to steal the joy I feel when they call. I'm not. Instead,

I'll make a call to a friend of mine in the same circumstance and we can compare notes on the latest grandchild giggles.

☀ *Step six: cultivate contentment by refusing to entertain "what might have been" thoughts.* Denise was having the time of her life. She loved snow skiing and going off on these brief weekend jaunts with her girlfriends—yes, even at fifty-plus years of age they continued to refer to one another as "girls"—it was good medicine. Denise thought back to her much younger days when she would go skiing with her then husband, and did they ever have fun! But that was before her divorce. Before her ex left her with a broken heart. The past, mingling pain with pleasure, would momentarily freeze Denise in her tracks. She would always recall their romantic getaway weekends whenever she first hit the ski slope, but she refused to allow her thoughts to linger there. Instead, Denise took in the day's scenery, the fresh air, the wintry fragrance of pine and fir. Then, just as she had in real life, Denise got moving. Leaving behind the past, she raced downhill exhilarated by every brush and turn along the way. Life was getting more exciting, Denise realized, and she felt freer than ever before.

☀ *Step seven: purposefully live for yourself and your loved ones.* After a second marriage ended in divorce, Gillian really didn't want to engage in life for a time. She was tired, disappointed, and wounded beyond repair. At least that's what she kept telling her friends. Wondering how she could ever trust another man—or if she even wanted to try—Gillian lived aloof, cut off, and isolated. Finally, after her best friend Kate figured Gillian had had enough time to grieve (they were that close as friends!), she gave her the straight scoop. Listen, Kate told her friend. You've endured a lot, I get that, but so have I, and I'm missing your company, so are your kids and grandkids. Life isn't just about your feelings. We need you to come back . . . now. Kate prepared for a hit, but Gillian just nodded . . . she got it too. No one anticipates life's hardships; no one asks for them. And no one better than a faithful friend who's also been bruised by its bumps to come alongside and goad another friend into moving ahead when the time is right.

 Step eight: focus on the eternal, not the temporal. Lydia got word that her cancer was back. She really couldn't grasp the news yet. It had been seven years since her left breast was removed. Lydia believed that her remission was a permanent thing. She was wrong. Who would have guessed after seven years of getting the "all clear" that a scan would reveal a reoccurrence? Lydia sat herself down in her favorite thinking chair, the one nearest the garden now full to overflowing with this summer's bounty. She thought about the ironies of life. The hurts and the losses. The joys and happiness. Lord, me again. Sitting here trying to figure out what You've got planned for me this time. I know, it's not for me to understand . . . but I wouldn't mind an extra measure of trust coming my way. You know Lord, I can't face this without You . . . yes, You know. You always do, and in your bounty I'll find my strength.

✺

Every Mother's Prayer

Lord,
Your love for me has been constant. That single word describes, de-
fines, and compels me to give You thanks after thanks for Your many
mercies. This life of mine is not over; the hardships I've endured have
made me into the woman I am today. Painful though each trial was,
I have to honestly look back and say I'm not full of regret and sorrow
for having walked this path. Yes, at times it was lonely and heart
breaking, and often I didn't believe I would have the strength to face
the next morning. But, with Your hand of grace and goodness, You
helped me. See better. Helped me recognize those small yet hopeful
signs that You were indeed working on my behalf. Feel encouraged.

By bringing friends to console and comfort me, You used them to wrap Your arms around me. Remain hopeful. The promises You offered me in Your Word gave me direction, purpose, and courage. I learned how to set my expectations on You alone, never on this world's goods or on its temporary, fleeting pleasures. You put within my heart a vision for eternity! I pray that every day, no matter what it brings, affords me continued opportunities to serve You better, honor you more, and trust You implicitly. Your life for mine. Now, my life is Yours. Amen.

Thought for the Day

"How we define faith, and what we expect from it, will lead either to a hope that is based in eternity or to a disillusionment that is based on ever-changing earthly circumstances. Disillusionment is born when we expect this world to be like the next, or when we try to live in this world without regard for the next. Self-centeredness shrinks our souls; even blessings can get boring. We need meaning, purpose, a mission, and a hope."

—*Authentic Faith: The Power of a Fire-Tested Life,* by Gary Thomas

Recommended Resources

Alsdorf, Debbie. *Deeper: Living in the Reality of God's Love*. Grand Rapids: Revell, 2008.

Fitzpatrick, Elyse & Laura Hendrickson, M.D. *Will Medicine Stop the Pain? Finding God's Healing for Depression, Anxiety, & Other Troubling Emotions*. Chicago: Moody, 2006.

Goodman, Karon Phillips. *Pursued by the Shepherd: Every Woman's Journey from Lost to Found*. Grand Rapids: Revell, 2007.

Guthrie, Nancy. *Holding On to Hope: A Pathway Through Suffering to the Heart of God*. Carol Stream, Ill.: Tyndale, 2006.

Ireland, David D. *Secrets of a Satisfying Life: Discover the Habits of Happy People*. Grand Rapids: Baker, 2006.

James, Carolyn Custis. *The Gospel of Ruth: Loving God Enough to Break the Rules*. Grand Rapids: Zondervan, 2008.

Julian, Larry. *God is My Success: Transforming Adversity into Your Destiny*. New York: Warner Faith, 2005.

Kent, Carol. *A New Kind of Normal: Hope-Filled Choices When Life Turns Upside Down*. Nashville: Nelson, 2007.

———. *When I Lay My Isaac: Unshakable Faith in Unthinkable Circumstances*. Colorado Springs: NavPress, 2004.

Kok, Elsa. *A Woman with a Past, A God with a Future: Embracing God's Transforming Love*. Birmingham, Ala.: New Hope, 2006.

Lotz, Anne Graham. *I Saw the Lord*. Grand Rapids: Zondervan, 2006.

———. *Just Give Me Jesus*. Nashville: Nelson, 2002.

McKinley, David H. *The Search for Satisfaction: Looking for Something New under the Sun.* Nashville: Nelson, 2006.

Ortberg, John. *When the Game is Over It All Goes Back in the Box.* Grand Rapids: Zondervan, 2007.

Peace, Martha. *Attitudes of a Transformed Heart.* Newburyport, Mass.: Focus, 2002.

Rhodes, Tricia McCary. *Intimate Intercession: The Sacred Joy of Praying for Others.* Nashville: Nelson, 2005.

Rinehart, Paula. *Better Than My Dreams: Finding What You Long for Where You Might Not Think to Look.* Nashville: Nelson, 2007.

Swindoll, Charles. *Job: A Man of Heroic Endurance.* Nashville: Nelson, 2004.

Thomas, Gary. *Authentic Faith: The Power of a Fire-Tested Life.* Grand Rapids: Zondervan, 2002.

―――. *Sacred Influence.* Grand Rapids: Zondervan, 2006.

Tripp, Paul David. *Lost in the Middle: Midlife and the Grace of God.* Wapwallopen, Pa.: Shepherd, 2004.

―――. *Age of Opportunity: A Biblical Guide to Parenting Teens.* Phillipsburg, N.J.: P&R, 2001.

―――. *Instruments in the Redeemer's Hands: People in Need of Change Helping People in Need of Change.* Phillipsburg, N.J.: P&R, 2002.

Vernick, Leslie. *How to Find Selfless Joy in a Me-First World.* Colorado Springs: WaterBrook, 2003.

West, Kari. *When He Leaves: Help and Hope for Hurting Wives.* Eugene, Ore.: Harvest, 2005.

248.8431 Howe, Michele.
HOW
         Still going it
         alone.

$14.95

DATE			

28
Day
Loan

DISCARD

BAKER & TAYLOR